BOOKS BY EDWARD HOAGLAND

Essay Collections

The Courage of Turtles
Walking the Dead Diamond River
Red Wolves and Black Bears

Travel

Notes from the Century Before:
A Journal from British Columbia

Novels

The Peacock's Tail
The Circle Home
Cat Man

RED
WOLVES
AND
BLACK
BEARS

RED WOLVES AND BLACK BEARS

EDWARD HOAGLAND

RANDOM HOUSE · NEW YORK

All rights reserved under International and Pan-American
Copyright Conventions. Published in the United States by
Random House, Inc., New York, and simultaneously in Canada
by Random House of Canada Limited, Toronto.

Library of Congress Cataloging in Publication Data
Hoagland, Edward.
Red wolves and black bears.
I. Title.
PS3558.0334R4   814'.5'4   75–40243
ISBN 0–394–40091–7

Acknowledgment is given to the magazines in which these essays, some-
times shortened, first appeared. "Lament the Red Wolf," "Bears, Bears,
Bears," and "A Low-water Man" were in *Sports Illustrated*. "Johnny
Appleseed, Bluegrass, Egg Creams," "Heroes and Footfalls," and one
section of "Apocalypse Enough" are from *The New York Times Maga-
zine*. (*Not Man Apart* published the other section.) "A Run of Bad
Luck" was in *Newsweek*, and "Virginie and the Slaves" in *Travel and
Leisure*. "Thoughts on Returning to the City," "Pathos and Perfection,"
"That Gorgeous Great Novelist," and "Nine Small (Literary) Truths"
appeared in *The Village Voice*. *The Saturday Review* published "Howl-
ing Back at the Wolves." "Writing Wild," "Where the Action Is," and
"But Where Is Home?" are from *The New York Times Book Review*.
"Dogs, and the Tug of Life" and "Other Lives" appeared in *Harper's*.
"City Walking" appeared in slightly different form in *The New York
Times Book Review*, © 1975 by The New York Times Company. Re-
printed by permission.

Manufactured in the United States of America

9 8 7 6 5 4 3 2

First Edition

FOR ARCHIBALD MacLEISH,

BRIGIT McCARTHY,

LEONORE COMORA AND

PETER HAMILL

CONTENTS

CONTENTS

AUTHOR'S NOTE

Sometimes part of the pleasure of a book of essays is to ignore the order in which they have been printed and skip around to suit oneself. This can still be done with the short pieces collected here, but since the longer ones have been expanded to lead into each other or echo back, they probably should be read as they appear.

RED
WOLVES
AND
BLACK
BEARS

THOUGHTS ON RETURNING TO THE CITY AFTER FIVE MONTHS ON A MOUNTAIN WHERE THE WOLVES HOWLED

City people are more supple than country people, and the sanest city people, being more tested and more broadly based in the world of men, are the sanest people on earth. As to honesty, though, or good sense, no clear-cut distinction exists either way.

I like gourmets, even winetasters. In the city they correspond to the old-timers who knew all the berries and herbs, made money collecting the roots of the ginseng plant, and knew the taste of each hill by its springs. Alertness and adaptability in the city are transferable to the country if you feel at home there, and alertness there can

3

quickly be transmuted into alertness here. It is not necessary to choose between being a country man and a city man, as it is to decide, for instance, some time along in one's thirties, whether one is an Easterner or a Westerner. (Middle Westerners, too, make the choice: people in Cleveland consider themselves Easterners, people in Kansas City know they are Western.) But one can be both a country man and a city man. Once a big frog in a local pond, now suddenly I'm tiny again, and delighted to be so, kicking my way down through the water, swimming along my anchor chains and finding them fast in the bottom.

Nor must one make a great sacrifice in informational matters. I know more about bears and wolves than anybody in my town or the neighboring towns up there and can lead lifelong residents in the woods, yet the fierce, partisan block associations in my neighborhood in New York apparently know less than I do about the closer drug-peddling operations or they surely would have shut them down. This is not to say that such information is of paramount importance, however. While, lately, I was tasting the October fruit of the jack-in-the-pulpit and watching the club-moss smoke with flying spores as I walked in the woods, my small daughter, who had not seen me for several weeks, missed me so much that when I did return, she threw up her arms in helpless and choked excitement to shield her eyes, as if I were the rising sun. The last thing I wish to be, of course, is the sun—being only a guilty father.

But what a kick it is to be back, seeing newspaperman

friends; newspapermen are the best of the city. There are new restaurants down the block, and today I rescued an actual woodcock—New York is nothing if not cosmopolitan. Lost, it had dived for the one patch of green in the street, a basket of avocados in the doorway of Shanvilla's Grocery, and knocked itself out. I'd needed to drag myself back from that mountain where the wolves howl, and yet love is what I feel now; the days are long and my eyes and emotions are fresh.

The city is dying irreversibly as a metropolis. We who love it must recognize this if we wish to live in it intelligently. All programs, all palliatives and revenue-sharing, can only avail to ease what we love into oblivion a little more tenderly (if a tender death is ever possible for a city). But to claim that the city is dying, never to "turn the corner," is not to announce that we should jump for the lifeboats. There are still no better people than New Yorkers. No matter where I have been, I rediscover this every fall. And my mountain is dying too. The real estate ads up in that country put it very succinctly. "Wealth you can walk on," they say. As far as that goes, one cannot live intelligently without realizing that we and our friends and loved ones are all dying. But one's ideals, no: no matter what currently unfashionable ideals a person may harbor in secret, from self-sacrifice and wanting to fall in love to wanting to fight in a war, there will continue to be opportunities to carry them out.

My country neighbor is dying right now, wonderfully fiercely—nothing but stinging gall from his lips. The wolves' mountain bears his name, and at eighty-six he is dying almost on the spot where he was born, in the one-room schoolhouse in which he attended first grade, to which he moved when his father's house burned. This would not be possible in the city. In the city we live by being supple, bending with the wind. He lived by bending with the wind too, but his were the north and west winds.

You New Yorkers will excuse me for missing my barred owls, ruffed grouse and snowshoe rabbits, my grosbeaks and deer. I love what you love too. In the city and in the country there is a simple, underlying basis to life which we forget almost daily: that life is good. We forget because losing it or wife, children, health, friends is so awfully painful, and because life is hard, but we know from our own experience as well as our expectations that it can and ought to be good, and is even *meant* to be good. Any careful study of living things, whether wolves, bears or man, reminds one of the same direct truth; also of the clarity of the fact that evolution itself is obviously not some process of drowning beings clutching at straws and climbing from suffering and travail and virtual expiration to tenuous, momentary survival. Rather, evolution has been a matter of days well-lived, chameleon strength, energy, zappy sex, sunshine stored up, inventiveness, competitiveness, and the whole fun of busy brain cells. Watch how a rabbit loves to run; watch him set scenting puzzles for the terrier behind him. Or a wolf's amusement at the anatomy of a deer. Tug, tug, he pulls out the long intestines: ah, Yorick, how *long* you are!

An acre of forest will absorb six tons of carbon dioxide in a year.

Wordsworth walked an estimated 186,000 miles in his lifetime.

Robert Rogers' Twenty-first Rule of Ranger warfare was: "If the enemy pursue your rear, take a circle till you come to your own tracks, and there form an ambush to receive them, and give them the first fire."

Rain-in-the-face, a Hunkpapa Sioux, before attacking Fort Totten in the Dakota Territory in 1866: "I prepared for death. I painted as usual like the eclipse of the sun, half black and half red."

HOWLING BACK
AT THE WOLVES

Wolves have marvelous legs. The first thing one notices about them is how high they are set on their skinny legs, and the instant, blurred gait these can switch into, bicycling away, carrying them as much as forty miles in a day. With brindled coats in smoky shades, brushy tails, light-filled eyes, intense sharp faces which are more focused than an intelligent dog's but also less various, they are electric on first sighting, bending that bushy head around to look back as they run. In captivity when they are quarreling in a cage, the snarls sound guttural and their jaws chop, but scientists watching pet wolves in the woods speak of their flowing joy, of such a delight in running that they melt into the woods like sunlight, like running water.

The modern study of American wildlife may be said to have begun with Adolph Murie, who, writing about the wolves of Mount McKinley in 1944, realized there was not much point in a scientist's shooting them; so few wolves were left that this would be killing the goose laying the golden eggs. In those days even the biologists dealing with animals which weren't considered varmints mainly just boiled the flesh off their heads to examine the knobs on their skulls, or opened their stomachs to see what they ate. The scrutiny of skulls had resulted in a listing of eighty-six species and subspecies of the grizzly bear, for example (it's now considered that there were a maximum of only two), and twenty-seven specified New World wolves (again, now revised down to two). Murie, in the field and looking at scats, could do a more thorough investigation of diet than the autopsy fellows, who, as it was, knew almost nothing else about the life of wolves.

Murie and Ian McTaggart Cowan in Canada were the best of the bedroll scientists. They could travel with dogs all winter in the snow or camp alone on a gravel bar in a valley for the summer, go about quietly on foot and record everything that they saw. No amount of bush-plane maneuvering and electronic technology can quite replace these methods, by which the totality of a wilderness community can be observed and absorbed. Young scientists such as L. David Mech, who has been the salvation of wolves in Minnesota, which is practically the only place in the lower forty-eight states where they still occur, try to combine the current reliance on radiotelemetry with some of that old bedroll faithfulness to the five senses shared by a man with the animals he is studying.

Big game, like elk and caribou, and big glamorous predators have naturally received first attention, people being as they are, so that much more is known about wolves than about the grasshopper mouse, though the grasshopper mouse is a wolf among mice, trailing, gorging upon small mammals and insects; in fact, with nose pointed skyward, it even "howls." On lists of endangered species you occasionally find little beasts that wouldn't excite much attention on a picnic outing, but despite all the talk about saving the fruits of two billion years' worth of evolution, the funds available go to help those animals that tend to remind us of ourselves—rhinos, whales, falcons—and there aren't many lists of endangered plants.

So it is that the predator specialists are predatory. A hawk man drops out of the sky for a visit; he has radios attached to assorted raptors and albatrosses and swans, and flies around the world to track their migrations. During his chat about perfecting antennas it is obvious that he is full of what in an animal he would call "displaced aggression." The scientist Albert Erickson, who has worked on grizzlies in the north and leopard seals in Antarctica, was known as "Wild Man Erickson" when he studied black bears in Michigan. The Craighead brothers, Frank and John—territorial, secretive and competitive—have been working on a definitive study of grizzlies (which are also territorial, secretive and competitive) for umpteen years, scrapping with the National Park Service at Yellowstone and embargoing many of their own findings in the meantime. Maurice Hornocker, who is now the definitive mountain-lion man and who trained with them, is just as close-mouthed—as close-mouthed as a mountain lion, indeed. Down in Grand Chenier, Louisiana, Ted Joanen, the state's alligator expert, is equally able and reserved. One doesn't understand right away why he happens to be devoting his life to learning more about alligators than anybody else, rather than ibises or chimney swifts or pelicans, until he gets to describing how alligators can catch a swimming deer, pull it under the water, drown it and tear its leg off by spinning like a lathe, and then points to one's own twitching leg.

Wolves *would* be more of a loss to us than some exotic mouse, because they epitomize the American wilderness as no other animal does, and fill both the folklore of childhood and that of the woods—folklore that would wither away if they all were to die, and may do so in any case. We know that the folklore was exaggerated, that generally they don't attack man, which is a relief, but we treasure the stories nonetheless, wanting the woods to be woods. In the contiguous states the gray wolf's range is less than one percent of what it used to be, and that patch of Minnesota wilderness, twelve thousand square miles where they live in much the same density as in primeval times, is greatly enriched by the presence of wolves.

Wisconsin didn't get around to granting its wolves protection until they had become extinct, but Mech got the Minnesota bounty removed and almost single-handedly turned local thinking around, until there is talk of declaring the wolf a "state animal" and establishing a sanctuary for it in the Boundary Waters Canoe Area. Mech is a swift-thinking, urbane, amused man, bald, round-faced, not a bit wolflike in appearance, although he is sharp in his rivalry with other scientists. As an advocate he knows how to generate "spontaneous" nationwide letter-writing campaigns and can gather financial support from the National

Geographic Society and the New York Zoological Society, from Minneapolis industrialists and the federal government. He has a soul-stirring howl, more real than reality, that triggers the wolves into howling back when he is afoot trying to locate them, but his ears have begun to dim from a decade or more of flying all winter in flimsy planes to spot them against the snow. Sometimes he needs an assistant along to hear whether a pack at a distance is answering him.

That wolves do readily answer even bad imitations of their howl may have a good deal of significance. Observers have noticed the similarities between the intricate life of a wolf pack and the most primitive grouping of man, the family-sized band. Often there is a "peripheral wolf," for instance, which is tolerated but picked on, and as though the collective psyche of the pack required a scapegoat, if the peripheral wolf disappears another pack member may slip down the social ladder and assume the role, or a stray that otherwise might have been driven off will be adopted. The strays, or "lone wolves," not being bound by territorial considerations, range much farther and frequently eat better than pack wolves do, but are always seeking to enroll themselves.

What seems so uncanny and moving about the experience of howling to wolves, then hearing them answer, may be the enveloping sense of déjà vu, perhaps partly subliminal, that goes right to one's roots—band replying to band, each on its own ground, gazing across a few hundred yards of meadow or bog at the same screen of trees.

The listener rises right up on his toes, looking about happily at his human companions.

Wolf pups make a frothy ribbon of sound like fat bubbling, a shiny, witchy, fluttery yapping, while the adults siren less excitably, without those tremulous, flexible yips, although they sometimes do break pitch into a yodel. The senior wolf permits the response, if one is made, introducing it with his own note after a pause—which is sometimes lengthy—before the others join in. Ordinarily pups left alone will not answer unless the adult closest to them does so, as he or she returns to protect them. Wolves howl for only a half-minute or so, though they may respond again and again after a cautious intermission, if no danger is indicated from their having already betrayed their position. Each wolf has a tone, or series of tones, of its own that blends into an iridescent harmony with the others, and people who howl regularly at a wolf rendezvous soon acquire vocal personalities too, as well as a kind of choral sequence in which they join together—cupping their mouths to the shape of a muzzle on cue.

I went out with a student of Mech's, Fred Harrington, who records and voice-prints wolf howls. His wife was along, doing the puppy trills, and so was the trap-line crew, who attach radio-collars to the wolves they catch. We stood at the edge of a cutover jack-pine flat, with a few tall spruces where the wolves were. The sun was setting, the moon was rising, squirrels and birds were chitting close by, and we knew that a radio-collared bear was digging its winter den just over the rise. Howling is not a hunting cry and does not frighten other animals. The wolves howled as if for their own edification, as a pleasurable thing, a popular, general occasion set off by our calls to them, replying to us but not led by our emphasis or interpretation. If they had been actively scouting us they would have kept silent, as they do in the spring when the pups are too young to travel. To us, their chorus sounded isolated, vulnerable, the more so because obviously they were having fun, and we all felt the urge to run toward them; but they didn't share that feeling. A pack needs at least ten square miles for each member, as well as a deer every eighteen days for that individual, or a deer every three days for a pack of six. The figure for moose is one every three days for a pack of fifteen, Mech has calculated. Thus, howling between packs does not serve the function of calling them to confabulate. Instead, it seems to keep them apart, defining rough boundaries for their separate ranges, providing them mutually with a roster of strength, though by howling, mates in a pack do find one another and find solidarity.

In Algonquin Provincial Park in Ontario thousands of people howl with the wolves in the early autumn. Whether or not it is a high point for the wolves, it certainly is for the people. I've gone to one of the favorite locations, where the ground is littered with cigarette butts, and tried, except the day was rainy and the wolves couldn't hear me. Nobody who has had the experience will fail to root for the beasts ever after. Glacier National Park in Montana is next to Canada, like Mech's country, and they may manage to become reestablished there; Yellowstone

Park has a small vanguard. In East Texas a few hundred survive, hiding in the coastal marshes. These are red wolves—relic relations of the gray wolf that inhabited the Southeast and lower Mississippi Valley and are probably now doomed, pushed up against the sea, with no reservoir such as the wildlands of Canada provide from which to replenish their numbers.

Apparently a special relationship can exist between men and wolves which is unlike that between men and any of the bears or big cats. One might have to look to the other primates for a link that is closer. It's not just a matter of howling; owls with their hoots and loons with their laughter also interact with wolves. Nor is it limited to the mystery of why dogs, about fifteen thousand years back, which is very recent as such events go, cut themselves away from other wolves by a gradual, at first "voluntary" process to become subservient to human beings as no other domestic creature is, running with man in packs in which *he* calls the tune. Another paradox is that the wolves which remained wolves, though they are large predators that might legitimately regard a man-shaped item as prey, don't seem to look upon him as such; don't even challenge him in the woods in quite the same way that they will accost a trespassing cougar or grizzly.

In the campaign to rescue the wolf from Red Riding-hood status, some scientists, including Mech, have over-done their testimonials as to its liberal behavior, becoming so categorical that they doubt that any North American wolf not rabid has ever attacked a human being. This does violence to scientific method, as well as to the good name

15

of countless frontiersmen who knew more about the habits of wilderness animals than it is possible to learn today. (What these scientists really mean is that none of their Ph. D. candidates doing field work has been attacked by a wolf so far.) Such propaganda also pigeonholes the wolf in a disparaging way, as if it were a knee-jerk creature without any options, like a blowfish or hog-nosed snake.

But the link with man remains. Douglas H. Pimlott, who is Canada's wolf expert, explores this matter in *The World of the Wolf*. He mentions behavioral patterns that are shared by man and wolf, and by indirection might have come to influence wolves. Both hunt cooperatively in groups and are nearly unique in that respect; both have lived in complex bands in which the adults of either sex care for the young. He mentions the likelihood that there are subconscious attributes of the human mind that may affect wolves. After all, the bonds between a man and dog penetrate far beyond the awe of the one for the other— are more compulsive, more telepathic than awe—and cannot be fully explained under the heading of love. Wolves, like dogs, says Pimlott, are excellent readers of signs because of their social makeup and their cruising system of hunting, which does not depend as much on surprise as the habits of most other predators do: "They instinctively recognize aggression, fear, and other qualities of mind which are evidenced in subtle ways by our expressions and actions. . . . In hunting we stalk deliberately, quietly . . . in winter we move through the woods and across lakes and streams deliberately, as a wolf does in traveling over his range, hunting for prey."

16

These movements indicate to wolves that we are superior predators—superior wolves—and not prey. It could be added that wolves, like dogs, take a remarkable delight in submissive ritual, ingratiating themselves, placating a bigger, more daring beast—this part of their adaptation through the millennia to life in a pack, in which usually only one or two members are really capable of killing the sizable game that will feed many mouths; the rest dance attendance upon them. Of course not only the fellow prowling in the woods is predatory. In the city, when much more driving and successful men emerge on the street for a business lunch, their straight-line strides and manner, "bright-eyed and bushy-tailed," would bowl over any wolf.

A

LOW-WATER

MAN

Leave the astronauts out
of it, and the paratroop teams that free-fall for 10,000
feet or skate down by means of those flattish, maneuver-
able new parachutes. Leave out the six people who have
survived the 220-foot fall from the Golden Gate Bridge,
and the divers of Acapulco, who swan-dive 118 feet, clearing outcrops of 21 feet as they plunge past the sea cliff.
Leave out even the ordinary high diver, who enters the
pool rigid and pointed after a comely jackknife. Come
down from such lofty characters to Henri LaMothe—who
on his seventieth birthday last April dove from a 40-foot
ladder into a play pool of water 12 inches deep.

The high diver in his development first increases his
height, then crowds more gainers and twists into his drop,
but LaMothe's progress in middle age and since has not
involved ascending higher. Rather, he has provided himself with less and less water to land in: an ambition oddly
private and untheatrical. Three feet, two feet, twenty
inches, sixteen inches, fourteen inches. He strikes, not

headfirst or feetfirst, which would be the finish of him, but on the arched ball of his belly. Inevitably, his endeavor over the years has been to manage somehow to jump into no water at all in the end. Since this is impossible, he is designing a break-away plastic pool whose sides will collapse as he hits, so that except for the puddles remaining on the pavement, he will at least experience the sensation of having done just exactly that.

It's as if LaMothe hasn't heard that during his lifetime man has learned to fly, or that he knows that the flying we do is not really flying. In the meantime his posture resembles a flying squirrel's. Apparently nobody else entertains similar ambitions, although one of the old-time carnival thrills was for a stunt man to jump feetfirst from a platform into a very considerably deeper hogshead of water, doing what divers describe as a tuck as he entered, then partly somersaulting and scooping madly. As the person dropped, he could steer just a bit by tilting his head—the head being the heaviest mass in the body—but like Henri's feat, this one was gilded with none of the nifty, concise aesthetics of fancy diving: no "points" to be scored, no springboard to bound from, no Hawaiian plunge after the mid-air contortions into a sumptuous, deep-blue, country-club pool, with a pretty crawl stroke afterwards to carry him out of the way of the next competitor. Such a performer lived on hot dogs and slept with the ticket seller and often received an involuntary enema through the two pairs of trunks that he wore; got sinus and mastoid infections and constant colds from the water forced into his nose.

LaMothe dives, however—doesn't jump—into water that

19

scarcely reaches his calves as he stands up, his hands in a Hallelujah gesture. His sailor hat never leaves his head, his back stays dry unless the wash wets him, and yet so bizarre is the sight of a person emerging from water so shallow that one's eye sees him standing there as if with his drawers fallen around his feet. As he plummets, his form is as ugly and poignant as the flop of a frog—nothing less ungainly would enable him to survive—and, watching, one feels witness to something more interesting than a stunt—a leap for life into a fire net, perhaps.

He wears a thin white-sleeved bodysuit that looks like a set of long johns (the crowd is likely to titter), and, up on his jointed ladder, huddles into a crouch, holding onto the shafts behind him. Like a man in the window of a burning building, he squats, stares down, hesitating, concentrating, seeming to quail, and finally letting go, puts out his arms in what seems a clumsy gesture, creeping into space between gusts of wind. He sneaks off the top of the ladder, spreading his fingers, reaching out, arching his back, bulging his stomach, cocking his head back, gritting his teeth, never glancing down, and hits in the granddaddy of all bellywhoppers, which flings water twenty feet out.

Though one's natural impulse when falling is to ball up to protect one's vitals, he survives precisely by thrusting his vitals *out*. He goes *splat*. And when a microphone is put to him—"How do you do it?"—Henri says, "Guts!" grinning at the pun. "Why do you do it?" asks the reporter. "I get a *bang* out of it!" sez LaMothe, sez that he is "a low-water man." In his long johns, white-haired, in that tremulous hunch forty feet up a guyed-out magnesium

20

ladder that he folds up and wheels about for fees of a few
hundred dollars, he's anything but an Evel Knievel. He's
from vaudeville, a fire victim, his career a succession of
happenstances.

In Chicago, growing up pint-sized with the nickname
Frenchy—his father, a South Side carpenter, was from
Montreal—he dove off coal tipples, bridges and boxcars,
swimming and swaggering at the 76th Street Beach, doing
the Four-Mile Swim off Navy Pier. In the winter he swam
indoors with a gang that included Johnny Weissmuller,
who was already swinging from the girders over the pool.
But Henri's hands were too small, his build too slight for
competitive swimming. To make a living he drove a cab
and posed at the Chicago Art Institute, where he began
to draw too. He stayed up late, speeding around town to
neighborhood Charleston contests, four or five in a night
—this being the Roaring Twenties—winning up to a hundred dollars an evening. He quit modeling in order to
Charleston full time, closing his act with handstands, back
bends and a belly-flop, sliding and rolling across the
waxed floor. His girlfriend's specialty was the split; she'd
kick him into his belly-flop, do the split over him and
"lift" him up with two fingers and dance on his stomach
as he leaned over backwards, balancing on his hands.
They were local champions, and by and by he invented
an Airplane Dance, his arm the propeller—"the Lucky
Lindy," for Lindbergh—which he claims was adapted
into the Lindy Hop. June Havoc and Gypsy Rose Lee's
famously stingy stage mama took him to New York City
as one of six "Newsboys" in their hoofer show, but he quit

to dance in a musical called *Keep It Clean.* By 1928 he was dancing at the Paramount as "Hotfoot Henri" ("Hotpants" backstage), usually planted among the ushers or as a dummy sax player in the orchestra pit when the show began. The clowning, pat repartee and belly-busters were right up his alley; on occasion he still will flop on his breadbasket into a puddle of beer at home to startle guests, or lie flat and lift his wife Birgit by the strength of his stomach muscles.

Although he'd been thankful to dancing for whisking him away from the Windy City and the life of a commercial artist drawing pots and pans for newspaper ads, after the 1929 crash he had to scratch for a job. He designed Chinese menus to pay for his meals, did flyer layouts for theaters and bands, and painted signs. He was art editor of the *Hobo News*, later the *Bowery News*, and tinkered, streamlining the stapler used everywhere nowadays, and inventing a "Bedroom Mood Meter" to post on the wall, like the ones sold in Times Square novelty shops. He got work drawing advertising for a Long Island plastics company, and actually prospered; even flew his own plane. Mushing down for a landing, he would think of the pratfalls he had performed in the Charleston contests and his belly-flops back on Muscle Beach, clowning his way to popularity.

Clowning on the board at the swimming club for the executives, he heard the suggestion that he ought to do it professionally, and so after a stint in a shipyard during World War II he went swimming with Johnny Weissmuller's troupe in Peru. Then he went to Italy with his own

water show, the "Aquats," in partnership with two girls, one
of whom, a Dane called Birgit Gjessing, became his wife.
Birgit had been an actress in Germany during the war, a
swimmer before that, and a puppeteer back home in Den-
mark, marking time after fleeing the collapse of the Reich.
She's a lean lady of fifty-seven with a quick expressive
face, a school counselor now, but she remembers playing
chess in a wine cellar near Mainz during the worst of the
bombing. At one point in 1944 she traded her winter coat
for a bicycle, thinking to swim the Rhine while holding it
over her head and then peddle on home.

Henri would emulate the dives the girls did and mess
everything up, or get into a race and be towed through
the water, roped to a car. He dressed as Sweet Pea or
Baby Snooks with a curl painted on his forehead. Wheeled
to the pool in a buggy by Birgit, dressed in a starchy
costume, he would scramble up on the high diving board
while his nurse underneath pleaded with him to climb
down. She would fall in, and he would pancake on top of
her, landing crisscross. He used break-off boards to make
his dive doubly abrupt, or wore a pullover sweater fifteen
feet long, which would still be unraveling as he stumbled backwards into his fall. In a beret, with his French
mustache, he'd put on blue long johns with rolled-up
newspapers over his biceps and a great cape and, calling
himself Stupor Man, bend "iron" bars and launch himself
on a mission of mercy from a high place, only to crash
on his belly into the water. He would "drown" and need
artificial respiration, but as the girls bent over him, would
squirt water at them from his mouth. Then, running to

apologize to Birgit, he would trip, belly-whop, and skid into her.

He wore low-necked bathing suits through which he could push his bay window, and sometimes to publicize the show would stand on his elbows on a building ledge, drinking coffee, eating a doughnut. Unfortunately it wasn't until both he and the century were into their fifties that his agent had sense enough to tip him off that the dive he was doing anyway as a water comedian would earn more money if done straight, so he speaks of those first twenty years of diving as "wasted." Then it was maybe another two thousand leaps before his seventieth birthday provided a gimmick to get him a *Daily News* centerfold and a spot on a David Frost show. For part of this long period he practiced commercial art in New York, but New Year's Eve would find him in Miami Beach dressed as the Baby New Year, poised in a third-floor hotel window as the clock tolled twelve, diving into "Lake Urine," the kiddie pool. He sprang out of trees, from flagpole yardarms and roofs—once from the ensign standard forty-seven feet up into two feet of water in the Westchester Country Club wading pool. Touring the country clubs, they "ate lentils," says Birgit. And always Henri looked a bit silly as he stood up, the water lapping at his shins: the less water the sillier.

Water shows are lumped with ice shows in the lower echelon of show business. The very term has a kiddie ring. Indeed, Birgit still shivers, remembering a week in Quebec when they had to perform in a hockey rink, paired with a skating follies, in water poured into a tank right on top of the ice. She wore a fish costume and executed finny undulations to the *Basin Street Blues,* but otherwise, as always, tried to get herself and the rest of the ballet swimmers out of the water at frequent intervals to remind the audience that they were really human, not fishy, in shape. Ice skaters have no such identity problem. Water, on the other hand, elemental, deep, somber, healing as it is, imparts a nobility to swimming which no ice show can match. With the mysterious oceans behind it, stretching around the world, water can be a powerful ally.

But Henri, leaping into a thin film of water, has sacrificed the majesty of the ocean to the bravery of his frog dive. Landing as he does, on the paunch, the craw, the crop, he loses the pretensions to dignity of mankind as well. It's raw, realer than drama, and tremendously poignant; it's his masterpiece, he says, in a life of inventing, which, even when he's been shabbily treated on the show-business scene, nobody has been able to steal away from him. He talks now of diving from the Eiffel Tower or the Leaning Tower of Pisa, combining this with his dream of diving at last into no water at all.

He's a short, plump, pigeonlike man who rubs his stomach continually, bends his back and bulges his chest. His look is matter-of-fact, like a man calculating practicalities, yet self-preoccupied, like one who knows pain and catastrophe. Though he dives on an empty stomach with lungs half filled, he lives by the bulge of his stomach. Clapping his hands, he will demonstrate how his arched back is the key to surviving. If air is trapped between the hands the clap is loud, but if one hand is convex the impact is muted. Just so, he explains, an air pocket under his belly would "split me right open." His belly is holding up fine, but his back is decidedly less limber; his scrapbook of photographs testifies to what a bend he could bring to his work only a decade ago. Offstage he looked the daredevil then, and back in the fifties, his two lady partners would give him a rubdown after his feat. Now, because of the slackening that old age effects on the best of bodies, except for his stern mouth and nose he looks more like a health nut maintaining his youth.

He has a fluffy ring of white hair around his bald head, and likes being up on his ladder—says that he's happy up there. His beloved round pool glows like a globe below him, even seeming to expand. He says that a power goes out from him to intimidate the water. "That water is going to take the punishment, not me." Kids always ask whether it hurts. "Why do you care if it hurts?" he asks them. At the Hampton, Virginia boat show, where I watched him leap, his dressing room was the aisle between the showers and toilets. Among other exercises he did his stretching drill holding on to a sink and swinging from the top of a toilet stall. "Coffee's working," he said, because emptying his bowels was part of the ritual so he would feel "clean," ready for the impact. He drank a cup half an hour before he climbed up the ladder, both as a laxative and to bring an alive feeling to his stomach. Women sometimes ask if he wears a jock strap, but "I just put my tail between my legs and go." After the evening act he celebrated with a swig of whisky, rippling his stomach anatomy to help it down as he used to do to amuse the students at the Chicago Art Institute. For five or six hours afterwards in his room at the Holiday Inn he let his nerves unwind with the aid of beer, while concocting a vegetable-fruit mix in his blender and soup pot, the day's one big meal.

Once when he was a young man LaMothe swam the St. Lawrence—something his father before him had done —fetching up at a convent, where the nuns hid their eyes. And once he was paid three-thousand dollars for a week at the San Antonio HemisFair, "banging my belly." Working shopping malls and sports shows, he carries his pool in a shopping bag; it's a flimsy low roll of fencing with a plastic liner which sways with the waves of the blow. (Again, Henri's agent had to wise him up to the hammy fact that the sides ought to be down as low as the water.) On his ladder he lets all other sights and sounds except the bull's-eye blur out. He crouches, "hoping for" rather than aiming for it, and lets go, putting his froggy arms out as his body falls. A team of accident experts from General Motors has tested him and concluded that he hits with the force of gravity multiplied seventy times; or, with his weight, 10,500 pounds.

So he does what the bigger kids couldn't do, long after they have given up their own specialties. And since the death wish of a daredevil who is seventy years old must be fairly well under control, perhaps the best explanation for why he continues is that this is what he is good at. Humiliation is a very good school for clowns, and, watching him, as with certain other notable clowns, one is swept with a tenderness for him as he lands, God's Fool, safe

27

and sound and alive once again. As with them, our fascination is enhanced because at the same time that he has sought our applause, he has seemed to try to obscure our appreciation, make the venture difficult for us to understand, and thereby escape our applause—a "low-water man."

BEARS,
BEARS,
BEARS

Bears, which stopped being primarily predatory some time ago, though they still have a predator's sharp wits and mouth, appeal to a side of us that is lumbering, churlish and individual. We are touched by their anatomy because it resembles ours, by their piggishness and sleepiness and unsociability with each other, by their very aversion to having anything to do with us except for eating our garbage. Where big tracts of forest remain, black bears can still do fairly well. The grizzly's prickly ego is absent in them; they are unostentatious woodland animals that stay under cover and do not expect to have everything go their way.

Grizzlies never did inhabit the forested East. They lived on the Great Plains and in the Rockies and Sierras, much of it open or arid country; apparently they are more tolerant than black bears of hot, direct sun. In such surroundings no trees were at hand for the cubs to flee to and the adults developed their propensity for charging an intruder. For their own safety too, the best defense was an assault, and until we brought our rifles into play they didn't trouble to make much distinction between us and other predators. They still are guyed in by instinct to an "attack distance," as the biologists call it, within which their likely first reaction is to charge, whereas if they perceive a man approaching from farther off, they will melt away if they can.

Bears have a direct, simple vegetarian diet supplemented by insects and carrion or fish, so they need less operating space than a wolf, which weighs only about one-fourth what a black bear weighs but must obtain for itself a classy meat meal. Nevertheless, according to several studies, black bears require from one to five square miles apiece just to gather their food, and units of at least fifty square miles of wilderness for their wanderings and social relations. In this day and age such a chunk has other uses too. Loggers will be cutting on parts of it, and boy scouts holding encampments, canoeists paddling the rivers, and hikers and hunters traipsing across. Black bears were originally found in every state but Hawaii, and still manage to survive in about thirty, if only in remnant numbers, so that they seem able to coexist. They are coated for living up on the windy ridges or down in the swamps and hollows, where even the snowmobilers can't get to them during the winter because they are under the snow, and they give promise of being with us for a long while.

Probably the most ardent investigator of black bears right now is Lynn Rogers, a graduate student at the University of Minnesota. He's thirty-four, red-bearded, crew-cut with a wife who used to teach English and two children, and he is another one of David's Mech's protégés. He works in Isabella (once called Hurry Up, until a leading citizen renamed it after his daughter), which is a logging village, a tiny crossroads with more bars than grocery stores, settled by "Finlanders," as they are called, in the Arrowhead region of northern Minnesota, now the Superior National Forest. The logging is fading as aspen grows up in place of the old stands of big pine, but the Forest Service plants red or white pine where it can (there is more jack pine, however), and the swamps are forested with black spruce. The lakeshores are pretty, with birch, cedar, red maple, fir and white spruce, and the whole place is bursting with bears. On a seven-mile stretch of highway near Rogers' headquarters thirty were shot in one year. This was before the townspeople became interested in his work; now they let the bears live.

Rogers is a two-hundred-pounder with a rangy build and a small-looking head, no more bearish than Mech's is wolfish. Though there are scientists who come to resemble the animals they study, more often they look like athletic coaches, animals being in some sense our behind-hand brothers and these the fellows who watch out for them. Rogers could well be a coach, except for the streak in him that makes him extraordinary. In the woods he moves at a silent trot, as only the rarest woodsmen do. His thoughts, insofar as they could be elicited in the week I lived with him, seemed almost exclusively concerned with bears— catching them, amassing more data on them. He seldom reads a newspaper or watches television, and likes to kid his wife about the "fairy tales" of literature which she taught in school. When he takes a day off, it's to snap pictures of beaver or to wait half the day in a tree for an osprey to return to its nest. He's lived only in Minnesota and Michigan—grew up in Grand Rapids—but once he did stop off in Chicago, when driving between the two states, to go to the natural history museum. If you ask what he'd like to do when his achievements are properly recognized, he says he'd want to stay in Isabella and study lynx or else fisher.

As he sits in a brooding posture at the kitchen table, his body doesn't move for long periods and he thinks aloud, not so much in actual words as with a slow series of ums and ahs that seem to convey the pacing of his thoughts. But he lectures nicely, full of his subject, and in the woods whatever is lummoxy drops away in that quickness, the dozen errands he's running at once— searching for a plant whose leaves will match the un- known leaves he has been finding in a given bear's scats, examining a local bear-rubbing tree for hairs left on the bark since his last check. If he's lost in his jeep in the tangle of old logging roads, he gets a fix on the closest radio-collared bear and from that figures out where he is. If he's near one of them and wants a glimpse, he lifts a hand- ful of duff from the ground and lets it stream lightly down to test the wind before beginning his stalk. When he's radio- tracking from the plane that he rents, he watches his bears hunt frogs, or sees one surprise a wolf and pounce at it. If a bear in a thicket hasn't moved since his previous fix and is close to a road or a house, he may ask the pilot to land, if they can, to see whether it has been shot. Then, on the ground again, suddenly he'll climb an oak tree to taste the acorns on top, spurting up the branchless trunk without any spikes, his hands on one side pulling against his feet on the other. Lost in the yellow fall colors, munching bear food, he shouts happily from the tree, "What a job this is, huh?"

Wildlife biology as a profession interests me. Like the law, my father's vocation, it's one I follow. It's a stepchild among the sciences, however—badly paid, not quite respected, still rather scattered in its thrust and mediocre in its standards, and still accessible to the layman, as the most fundamental, fascinating breakthroughs alternate with confirmation of what has always been common knowledge—akin to that stage of medical research that told us that cigarettes were, yes, "coffin nails," and that frying foods in fat was bad for you. Partly because of its romantic bias, as a science wildlife biology has a tragic twist, since the beasts that have attracted the most attention so far are not the possums and armadillos that are thriving but the same ones whose heads hunters like to post on the wall: gaudy giraffes and gorillas, or mermaid-manatees, or "same-size predators," in the phrase ethologists use to explain why a grizzly bear regards a man thornily. It's not that the researchers have hurried to study the animals which are disappearing in order to glean what they can, but that the passion that activates the research in the first place is the passion which has helped hound these creatures off the face of the earth. Such men are hunters *manqué*.

Game wardens are also that way, but have the fun of

stalking, ambushing and capturing poachers, while so often the biologist sees his snow leopards, his orangutans, his wild swans and cranes, vanishing through change of habitat right while his study progresses—wondering whether his findings, like other last findings, invulnerable to correction though they soon will be, are all that accurate. Anthropology can be as sad a science when limited to living evidence and a primitive tribe, but the difference is that woodcraft itself is guttering out as a gift, and apart from the rarity now of observers who can get close to a wilderness animal which has not already been hemmed into a reserve, there is the painful mismatch of skills involved in first actually obtaining the data and then communicating it. Scientific writing need only be telegraphic to reach a professional audience, but again and again one runs into experts who have terrible difficulties in setting down even a small proportion of what they know. Eagerly, yet with chagrin and suspicion of anybody with the power to do the one thing they wish they could do (suspicion of city folk is also a factor), they welcome television and magazine reporters and interrogators like me, sometimes in order to see their own stories told, but sometimes to try to help save the animals dear to them—as if our weak words might really succeed.

But we observers have a piece missing too; maybe we put on our hiking boots looking for it. Like some of the wildlife experts—or like Lady Chatterley's gamekeeper, who was in retreat when he went into the woods—we don't entirely know why we are there. Not that an infatuation with wild beasts and wild places does us any

harm or excludes the more conventional passions like religion or love, but if I were to drive by a thicket of
palmettos and chicken trees way down South and you told
me that a drove of wild razorback hogs lived back in
there, I'd want to stop, get out, walk about, and whether
or not the place was scenic, I'd carry the memory with me
all day. It's said of a wilderness or an animal buff that
he "likes animals better than people," but this is seldom
true. Like certain pet owners, some do press their beasties
to themselves as compresses to stanch a wound, but others
are rosy, sturdy individuals. More bothersome to me is the
canard that *when I was a man I put away childish things,*
and I can be thrown into a tizzy if a friend begins teasing
me along these lines. (A sportswriter I know has gone
so far as to consult a psychiatrist to find out why a grown
man like him is still so consumed by baseball.) Rooting
around on riverbanks and mountain slopes, we may be
looking for that missing piece, or love, religion and the
rest of it—whatever is missing in us—just as we so often
are doing in the digging and rooting of sex. Anyway,
failure as a subject seems more germane than success at
the moment, when failure is piled atop failure nearly
everywhere, and the study of wildlife is saturated with
failure, both our own and that of the creatures themselves.

Rogers is a man surpassingly suited to what he is doing. Like me—it linked us immediately—he stuttered and
suffered from asthma when he was a child, and he's still
so thin-skinned that he will talk about suing a TV station
because it has edited his comments before airing them.

But with these thick-skinned bears—pigs-of-the-woods— he is in his element. Just as it was for me while I stayed with him, each day's busy glimpses and face-offs fulfilled his dream as a boy twenty or twenty-five years ago: to track and sneak close to, capture and fondle a noisy, goofy, gassy, hairy, dirty, monstrous, hot, stout, incontrovertible bear.

For their part, the bears have been *engineered* to survive. Whereas wolves have their fabulous legs to carry them many miles between kills, and a pack organization so resilient that a trapped wolf released with an injured paw will be looked after by the others until it is able to hunt again, a bear's central solution to the riddle of how to endure is to den. Denning does away with the harsh months of the year and concentrates the period when a bear needs to eat a lot in the harvest months when food is at hand. Although its breathing and heart rate slow by one half, and its metabolism subsides so that it loses only about five percent of its weight a month (half the rate at which it would shed weight during ordinary sleep), its temperature doesn't fall much while it is in the den. This distinguishes bears from bona-fide hibernators like bats and woodchucks, and means that they can give birth in the security of the den and can defend them- selves if attacked. The bear's sense of danger is reduced, so that the carefully surreptitious visits Rogers makes in midwinter go off with a minimum of fuss, but in its easily defended hole it can deal even with a pack of wolves.

Males sleep alone, but a sow has the company of her cubs—generally two or three. They are born around the end of January and den with her again the following winter; then in June, when they are a year and a half old, she permits a brawly big male, often several in sequence, to disrupt the close-knit life that she and the cubs have enjoyed since they were born. He or she drive them off and roam a bit together for a week or two, but by the device of delayed implantation of the ova her new cubs are not born till the middle of winter, which gives her a respite. The cubs are exceedingly little when they do arrive, weighing just over half a pound apiece—half what an infant porcupine weighs. The porcupine possesses quills, open eyes and other faculties to meet the world, whereas a bear cub has a great deal of developing to do in the dark den. Its eyes won't open for forty days, and small as it is, it isn't a drain on its fasting mother when suckling. Like a baby ape, it has a long interlude ahead of intimate association with her, an intimacy that will help make it far more intelligent than most animals.

Bears scrape out a depression for themselves under a pile of logs, a ledge or fallen tree, usually pulling in a layer of dead grass and leaves for insulation (paying a high price in heat and weight loss if they don't—one of the facets of denning that Rogers is studying). Some woodsmen claim that bears will position the entrance to face north in order to postpone the moment in the spring when meltwater chills them and forces them outside before the snow is gone and much food has become available. Emerging in mid-April, the adults look in fine shape; with their winter fur they even appear fat, though they shrivel rapidly during those first weeks as they tramp about trying to find something to eat—as if the fat cells are already empty and simply collapse. In Minnesota they break a path to the nearest aspen stand and climb or ride down the young trees to bite off the catkins at the tips of the limbs. They sniff out rotten logs under the snow and bash them apart, licking up the insects that have been hibernating there. A mother will take her cubs to a tall tree, such as a pine, and install them on the warm mound of earth at its base in a resting spot which she scrapes on the south side, nursing them and sending them scurrying up the trunk whenever she goes off in search of a meal. Then when the horsetails and spring grass sprout, the family begins to thrive.

The coating of fat that bears wear most of the year— and which was the frontiersman's favorite shortening— is of indirect use to them if they are shot, blocking the flow of blood, making them difficult to trail. Their flat feet, too, leave less of a track than the sharp feet of other game. Altogether they are excellently equipped, and if they don't insulate their dens or choose a sensible location for themselves, they'll probably come through the winter all right anyhow; the snow, melting to ice from the heat of their bodies, freezes into an igloo around them, complete with a breathing hole. If the complicated physiology by which they are supposed to fatten at an accelerated rate in the fall doesn't take hold (sometimes a mother gives so much milk that she stays thin), they muddle through even so, just as orphaned cubs do if they must winter alone without any denning instruction. The only dead bear Rogers has ever found in a den was a nineteen-year-old female, which despite this exceptionally advanced age, had given birth to two cubs. They had milk in their stomachs but apparently had been killed during her death throes.

In the past four years* Rogers has visited a hundred and six dens, first observing the bears' autumn rituals and later crawling inside. He has an advantage over his friend Mech simply because bears do den; he can head right for any bear wearing a functioning radio—in 1972 there were twenty-seven of them—and, after tranquilizing it, attach new batteries, which with luck are good till the following winter. He can outfit the yearlings with radios before they leave their mothers, and the habit of denning makes bears of any age easier to trap. His traps consist of two 55-gallon barrels welded together and baited with meat; far from finding the contraptions claustrophobic, the bears crawl comfortably in. Occasionally, when an animal is too bulky for the trap—as happened last summer when Rogers was trying to recapture a 455-pound bear whose collar had been torn off in a mating-season imbroglio—he sets foot snares at its favorite dump. This involves choreographing where the bear should place its feet by putting tin cans and other junk and branches close about the trap along its path. The snares are an unerring type developed in Washington State, where for some unfathomed reason

* I.e., as of 1972. I have not tried to incorporate his more recent findings, partly not to steal any thunder from his own presentation of them. My account here is deliberately anecdotal, incomplete and imprecise, so as to be scientifically useless whenever it does not cover fairly familiar ground.

(they seldom do it elsewhere) bears tear apart young trees to eat the cambium lining the inner bark, and the timber companies have declared war on them.

By comparison, Mech's wolves are will-o'-the-wisps. From an airplane a frustrated Mech may see one of them wearing a collar whose radio went dead years ago. Even Maurice Hornocker, the mountain-lion man, who works in Idaho, has a simpler time of it because his subjects, while they would be just as hard as a wolf to catch with an ordinary steel trap, obligingly leap into a tree in the winter, when snowed into a valley and pursued by hounds, where he shoots them with a tranquilizing dart and, climbing up, lowers them gently on the end of a rope as the drug takes effect. The best that can be said for wolves in this respect is that at least they do howl morning and evening in certain seasons, and are sociable souls, so that to keep tabs on one is to know the activities of five or ten others.

A heat scientist who is collaborating with Rogers in studying the biology of denning hopes to insert a scale underneath a wild bear so that a continuous record can be obtained of the rate at which it loses weight, to be collated with the winter's weather—weight loss being heat loss in this case, since the bear neither eats nor excretes. Another scientist in Minneapolis, a blood chemist, is creating from the unprecedentedly wide sampling of bears' blood that Rogers has sent him a profile of its composition, by season and in relation to sex, age, body temperature, sickness or behavioral peculiarities. In concert, they are studying particularly the breakneck conversion of food to fat during the late summer, and a nutritionist will analyze the many foods the bears eat. Rogers has charted their diet through the year, drawing on the evidence of scats, his walks and sightings from the air and their radioed locations. The scats he sifts in a pan of water. Leaves, wasp heads and carrion hair float to the top; seeds, tinfoil and twigs sink to the bottom. He's also investigating the fine points of telling an animal's age by counting the rings in a cross section cut from a tooth. Like the rings in a tree, a dark annulus is deposited in the cementum every winter while the bear sleeps and a light one during the bright part of the year. The live-bear biologists pull out a lower premolar and the dead-bear biologists take a canine, but there are also false annuli to confuse the count.

Wildlife biology used to be rather hit-or-miss. Rogers' predecessors would hogtie a trapped bear once in a while and clap an ether cone on it, then proceed to take weights and measurements. From dead bears they catalogued parasites, and looked for placental scars on the uterus. Sometimes a bear was caught and tagged to see where it would travel before a hunter shot it, or it might be color-marked so that it could be recognized at a distance, and transported and released somewhere else to see whether it "homed." To maintain sovereignty, every state's game department insisted on going over much the same ground with these prankish experiments; more seriously, a study of bear depredations on livestock, if any, would be made, because the stereotype of bears as menacing varmints had to be discredited before the legislature could be persuaded to remove the bounty on them, forbid killing them in their dens and give them the spring and summer protection that animals regarded as game receive. In state after state it would be pointed out that back in 1943 California had declared the grizzly its "state animal," but by then twenty years had already elapsed since the last grizzly had vanished from the state. Arkansas and Louisiana set out to right the violence of the past by importing several hundred Minnesota black bears at a cost of up to six hundred dollars apiece. A few have sneaked into neighboring states to delight the outdoorsmen and give the pig farmers the willies (for it's no legend that bears relish pigs), and so Mississippians have had cause to wonder and whoop at the sight of bear prints in the mud, for the first time since back in the era when Faulkner wrote his masterpiece *The Bear.*

In the late 1950s tranquilizers began to be employed, then radio collars. A woodchuck in Maryland bore the first such device; now even turtles and fish are saddled with transmitting equipment, and there is talk of substituting a microphone for the beep signal in the case of certain outspoken creatures like wolves, to record their life histories vocally. Some experts distrust such tools, suspecting that the hallucinogen in the tranquilizer, the obtrusive handling of the animal while it is immobilized, and having to wear an awkward collar may alter its personality and fate. But Rogers is a believer. In Minnesota he has captured a hundred and eighty-three different bears, some many times—one a day during the peak of the summer. Earlier, in Michigan, he had assisted in catching about a hundred and twenty-five. Flying four hundred hours in 1972, as much as his budget allowed, he totted up more than three thousand fixes on his bears. Of the thirty-seven he had put radios on during the previous winter, he could still monitor eighteen in late September and locate nine others whenever he wished to pay his pilot extra for a longer search. One of the travelers, a three-year-old male he had first tagged in its mother's den, went clear to Wisconsin, nearly a hundred and fifty miles, before it was shot.

To place all this in perspective, the State of New Hampshire, for instance, until recently had only one bear trap, a converted highway culvert that was trundled out three or four times a year. The game wardens got so excited when it was used that two of them would sleep overnight in a station wagon parked close by so as to be there when the door clanged. Before Rogers' program began, the most sophisticated telemetric figures on black-bear territoriality had been drawn from the State of Washington, where seventeen bears had been radio-located four hundred and eighteen times from the ground.*

At Rogers' cottage the phone rings with reports of sightings, friends recognizing his ear tags and collars; everybody keeps an eye out the window in the evening for bears crossing the fields around Isabella. He likes these neighbors and talks endlessly—bears, bears, bears—and

---

* The Craighead brothers, however, who began their grizzly studies in Yellowstone Park in 1959, have captured altogether more than five hundred and fifty grizzlies.

his wife Sue loyally wears shirts with big bear tracks painted on them. She's witty, slightly conspiratorial, and a great help to him, pushing him as she might urge on a student of hers who was talented but disorganized. The data keeps pouring in because he has such a network of methods set up to collect it, and he's out gathering more every day besides. One has the feeling that without her the study might strangle in congestion. He mentions an expert he knew in Michigan who in the course of a decade had collected more information on bears than any other man there, but who, as the years went on, could never write down what he'd learned and get credit for it. Finally, to cushion his disappointment, his chief transferred him to the task of collecting a whole new raft of raw data on deer.

Rogers has received a modicum of funding from the state's Department of Natural Resources, the federal Forest Service, the National Rifle Association and other disparate groups. Mostly, though, it is some Minneapolis magnates who call themselves the Big Game Club who have backed him, and particularly a poker-faced department-store owner named Wally Dayton, who will drive up, go along on a tour with the enthusiastic Rogers, see a few bears, and head back toward the Twin Cities without a hint of his own reactions, except that shortly thereafter the university will get a contribution earmarked for his work. At first, in my time with him, it had seemed sadly chancy to me that he had been afforded so little official support for a project I knew to be first-rate. But soon such a sense evaporated; rather, how lucky it was that this late-blooming man, who creeps through the brush so consummately that he can eavesdrop on the grunting of bears as they breed, had discovered at last, after seven long years as a letter carrier in his hometown, what it was that he wanted to do! In his blue wool cap, with Santa Claus wrinkles around his eyes because of the polar weather he's known, shambling, blundering, abstracted at times, he is an affecting figure, a big Viking first mate proud of the fact that he can heft a 240-pound bear alone. He kisses his wife as he starts out, one pocket full of his luncheon sandwiches, the other with hay-scented packets of scats he forgot to remove after yesterday's trip (they smell pleasant enough, and he likes carrying them as boys like carrying snakes).

In grammar school, with his breathing problems, he couldn't roughhouse and was kept indoors—the teacher would give him a chance to tell the rest of the class what birds he had spotted out the window while they had been playing. As his asthma improved, he and a friend named Butch used to jump from tree to tree or swing on long ropes like Tarzan, until Rogers took a bad fall and was hospitalized. They swam in the summer, plunging into deep ponds and kicking their way underwater along the turtle runways on the bottom to go after snappers, whose meat they sold in Grand Rapids for a dollar a pound. They would never leave off exploring any pond where the fishermen told them there was an oversized fish until they'd determined whether or not it was a great six-foot pike. He still laughs remembering the times when it turned out to be nothing more than a carp.

In adolescence his stutter was the difficulty and he took extended solitary fishing trips. Boyish, he once went through an entire winter in Michigan without wearing an overcoat to see whether he could tough it out, having read of a man who went into the woods stark naked one fall to find out if he could clothe himself with skins and prevail. He was a colorful postman not only because of stunts like this but because hordes of dogs congregated about him on his rounds, following him for hours; in the afternoon sometimes he carried the little ones home in his pouch. He did some judo and boxing in gyms and got into street fisticuffs; he still likes to step into a fight where the odds are three or four against one and knock all the bullies out. Even after he had returned to college and met his wife and started studying bears, Rogers almost lost a finger when some bear feces got into a cut and he refused to go to a doctor at first. Only recently he inflicted what he is afraid may have been a permanent strain on his heart by racing through a swamp after an athletic bear scientist who makes it a point to always keep up with his hounds.

One might speculate that like Jack on the Beanstalk, he *has* to be boyish to be so indefatigable at sneaking up next to these furry ogres. He speaks proudly of his two plane crashes while out spotting bears; his one mishap when a bear chewed him occurred when he was working in front of a high school class with an underdosed bear that climbed to its feet and staggered off, and he was so embarrassed that he tried to wrestle it down. Like a denizen of the woods, he seems full of anomalies to an outsider. He was a Vietnam hawk and hippie-hater during the war, but was glad not to serve in the army himself when his asthma offered him a chance to stay out. He's a member of Zero Population Growth and is thinking of getting a vasectomy, yet kept asking me what it was like to live in New York; didn't the girls smoke an awful lot and wear too much makeup? Though he is working on his doctoral thesis, only lately has he entered what he calls a transitional stage away from his parents' fundamentalist beliefs. He went to a Baptist parochial school and junior college, and not till he went to Michigan State, after the mail-carrying years, did he encounter a serious argument against the theory of life propounded in Genesis. Taught Darwinism for the first time, he had to learn to stop raising his arm in astonishment in biology class and quoting the Bible. The teacher was nonplussed and would suggest "See me afterwards," but then would avoid the meeting, and the students naturally thought he was funny. Offended, Lynn also postponed matching up his parents' ideas with the rest of the world's. He was superb at bear-catching, after all, and felt he was working at real biology, not bookish stuff, and because he was keeping his thoughts to himself, when he did argue about evolution it was usually just as a doubting Thomas with a more convinced fundamentalist, not with a scientist who might have had it out with him. He still seems to be waiting for the rejoinders which never came when they should have, to explain things for him.

"Darwin is full of holes too, you know," he said to me in the jeep, looking to see whether I'd answer, but I smiled and shrugged. For years he and his friend Butch, swimming, leaping from tree to tree, had lived with the dream of Tarzan in their minds, but it was just Butch who had been allowed to go to the movies. He would come back after the show and tell Lynn about Tarzan's feats.

On one of our mornings together, a caller notified Lynn that a bunch of grouse hunters had pumped enough bird-shot into a bear caught in one of his foot snares to kill it, so he went out to do an autopsy. It was a mother with milk in her udders and two surviving cubs which had run away. She was brownish compared to an Eastern black bear but blacker than many Western bears. Her feet were cut from stepping on broken glass while garbage-picking, and years before her right ear had been torn off. While he worked, the hunters who had shot her showed up, hoping to claim the skin. They were rough, heavyset customers, one a battered-looking Indian, and the witnesses to the killing, who were also grouse hunters and were standing around in hopes that *they* might get the skin, were too scared to speak up until after the culprits had left—which they did just as soon as they heard Rogers talking about getting the law after them. Then when the witnesses, two St. Paul men, after he'd helped tie the gutted bear onto their car, felt safe enough to enlighten him, Rogers could scarcely believe his ears, that people were so chicken-hearted. He hollered at them, threatening to take the bear back, went to a phone and called all the game wardens around.

We drove to several other dumps—perhaps a desolate sight to most people, but not to him. Gazing up at the white gulls and black ravens wheeling above, he imitated how his bears weave their heads, looking up at the birds. He told cheery stories, wretched stories. Somebody in Isabella had gutshot a bear with a .22, and the beast took five months to die, at last going from den to den in the middle of winter, in too much pain to be able to sleep. It died in the open snow, its belly bloated with partly digested blood, having shrunk down to ninety pounds.

That afternoon David Mech's crew from Ely delivered one of his radioed bears, #433, which had been caught in one of their wolf traps. They'd already tranquilized it, and he treated its banged paw; "Poor 433, poor 433." He marked down the latest data on it and drove it back to its home territory. Sometimes he howls to a pack of Mech's wolves for the fun of it until they answer him, and has caught about twenty wolves in bear snares, enjoying his own mystic moments with them. He uses a choker on the end of a stick while he tapes their jaws and wraps a weighing rope around their feet, careful not to let them feel actually in danger of strangling, however, or they go mad. Crouched over them, he achieves an effect similar to that of a dominant wolf; the thrashing animal gives up and lies quietly. Sometimes a possumlike catatonia slips over it and it loses consciousness for a while.

The next day, because one of the newly orphaned cubs had been caught in a snare, he had a chance to tag it in order to keep track of its fortunes. Thanks to the marvelous alimentary system bears have, young orphans tend to stay fat, and they hang together through their first winter, but with no mother to defend a territory for them, many questions remain about how they eventually fit into the pecking order of the area. All summer he had been in radio contact with two cubs a poacher had orphaned in June, when they were not long out of their mother's den. They'd been keeping body and soul together, traveling cross-country in a haphazard fashion, presumably scuttling up a tree if a wolf or another bear materialized, until a Duluth, Missabe and Iron Range Railway train killed them. They had begun by eating their mother; maybe could not have survived otherwise, since they were un-weaned. One can imagine them at first simply scratching at her udder in order to reach the milk curdling inside.

In a barrel trap Rogers had caught a three-year-old male, blowing like an elephant because of the resonance of the barrels. Bears really can huff and puff enough to blow the house down. While it chuffed at him through one vent he injected the drugs Sernylan and Sparine into its shoulder through another, then lifted the door and rubbed the bear's head as it went under, boyishly showing me that he could. This was unfortunate because the bear's last waking image was of that dreaded hand. Licking its nose and blinking and nodding while the shot took effect, it kept its head up, straining, sniffing as though it were drowning, or like a torture victim struggling for air. Once Rogers live-trapped seven bears in a single day, and once in the winter he handled five bears in one den—four yearlings and their mama. He says that in his experience

all really large bears are males, though a hunter sometimes thinks he has shot a "big sow" because the males'
testicles retreat into their bodies after the breeding
season.

Later he shot a grouse for his supper, and showed me a
few empty dens, of the ninety-four he has located so far.
We drove to a bleak little hamlet called Finland to check
on bear #320, a sow he had already pinpointed more than
two hundred times in his studies of territoriality. She goes
there every fall to eat acorns, staying till the snow is
thick before hurrying twenty-odd miles back to her home
stamping ground to dig her den. "What a job!" he said
again, exuberantly showing me balm of Gilead, climbing
an oak tree or two, pointing out a dozen different kinds of
birds, and halting by the road to jump up on the roof of the
jeep and do a sweep with his antenna to see whether
another bear was near.

In a typical day for as much as six hours he will jounce
along abandoned logging trails, then go up with his
pilot for another four hours, the plane standing on one
wing most of the time in tight circles over a succession
of bears. Cautious pilots cost the project money, but he
has found a young man who is paying for his plane with
bear-study money and is daring enough. Wearing a head-
set, homing in according to the strength of the beeps en-
tering each ear, Rogers directs him by hand signals.
Sometimes the beeps sound like radar chirps, sometimes
like the *pop-pop-pop* of a fish-tank aerator. On the ground
they are still more accurate, to the point where he can

distinguish not only a bear's movements across humpy terrain but its restlessness during a thunderstorm, its activity pawing for ants, or digging its den.

These bears produce more cubs than the mothers of Michigan, which ought to signify that they eat better; yet the cubs seem to grow slower. Rogers tabulates the temperatures for each week of the summer, believing that the weather may be as important a factor as the availability of food. At the end of a hot summer with plenty of blueberries, the first-year cubs he was in touch with weighed only an average of thirty-two pounds, but another year, when there were practically no blueberries but the temperature was cooler, another group had managed to fatten to an average of forty-seven pounds. An older bear once expanded from eighty-nine to two hundred and fifty-five pounds in a year, and another gained ninety-five pounds in forty-two days, ending up at three hundred and eighty, and nevertheless crawled into a barrel trap, getting so stuck that Rogers had to stand the barrels on end and lift them off to free the poor fatty.

Despite these gourmand triumphs and the fact that his bears face little hunting, Rogers finds that the average age of the population is only about four and a half—just about the same as biologists calculate for much more severely hunted places like Vermont, where almost a quarter of the bears are shot every fall. Even without the attrition from hunting, the mortality among cubs, and more especially among yearlings and two-year-olds, is high. Nobody has quite figured out what happens to them. G. A. Kemp, a researcher at Cold Lake, Alberta, has theorized that the population is regulated mainly by the adult boars, which kill the subadults if there is a surplus. The Craigheads, working with the grizzlies of Yellowstone, have suggested that dominant bears—grizzlies that occupy themselves principally with being king of the hill around a dump or other gathering point, rather than with eating—seem to lose the will to live when defeat comes, and fade from the scene.

Bears don't mature sexually until they are four, which, combined with the circumstance that the sows only breed every other year, and plenty of eligible sows not even then, gives them one of the lowest reproductive capabilities of any animal. Now that his research has extended through several years, however, bears that Rogers handled as infants, then watched play on their mothers' backs, are themselves giving birth. Occasionally he tracks them for a full twenty-four hours, using student assistants, discovering when they travel and how far and fast. In this wild region, they do most of their sleeping in the dark of the night, from midnight to five.

From his plane in the fall he photographs the terrain in color so as to delineate the zones of vegetation, mapping these to compare with his radio-marked bear ranges for the same area. Keying the bears to the vegetation indicates the feed and habitat they prefer, and also which logging practices of the past have benefited them. Logging, like a forest fire or a tornado, brings in new growth, and even in the primitive section of the national forest, where cutting is not allowed, bears haunt the openings where vetch and pea vine have had an opportunity to sprout and where the windfallen trees are dry from the sun and teem with bugs. On the other hand, clear-cutting does them no good because, like other game animals, they are uncomfortable without hideouts nearby. Sometimes the Forest Service, adding insult to injury, sprays on a herbicide to kill the young aspens and birch—the trees here which are most palatable to wildlife; Rogers is on the watch for any birth defects in his new cubs that may result.

In the spring and early summer the bears' diet is salady —early greens in shady places, and clover, grass, plantains, pea vine and vetch. They dig out grubs, chipmunks and burrowing hornets, clean up wolf kills, eat dandelions, strawberries (the first of the berries), juneberries, bilberries, thimbleberries, chokeberries, chokecherries, rose hips, haw apples, wild plums, hazelnuts and osier dogwood. Raspberries, although abundant, are not eaten in the quantities one might imagine, perhaps because they grow singly on the cane, but bears do feast on blueberries in midsummer, pausing only for a week or two to give closer attention to the berries of the wild sarsaparilla plant. In Michigan and New England they stay above ground into November, munching nuts in the hardwood forests and apples in derelict orchards, but in Rogers' wilderness the last crop eaten is the fruit of the mountain ash—red, berrylike clusters. By October most of the bears have chosen their dens and are puttering around—they excavate less than grizzlies—sleeping more and more, gradually letting their bodies wind down, except for a few savvy males which journey to Lake Superior to visit the dumps at the resorts there, eating until the snow covers their food before making tracks back. The Craigheads, indeed, think that grizzlies may possess an instinct to enter their pre-dug dens during a storm, when the snow will cover their tracks. When a bear stops eating and its intestines are empty, a seal of licked fur, pine needles and congealed digestive juices forms across the anus, putting a period to the year.

Usually they are tucked in their dens before the first harsh cold snap. The cold itself doesn't affect them except to put hair on their chests, but once the food supply is blanketed over, their interests are best served by going to sleep. During the winter their tapeworms starve to death and their cubs have maximum protection, and, for the rest of the year, they generally give every evidence of invulnerability to natural disaster because of the array of foods that suit them. In 1972, for example, when a June frost had ruined both the blueberry and mountain-ash crops, the Isabella bears needed to improvise an unsugary diet of salads right into the fall, then ran out of fodder entirely a month earlier than usual; yet when they denned they wore the same good belting of fat.

Disease, too, like malnutrition, is uncommon among bears; their preference for solitude helps ensure that. One of the mysteries that have intrigued biologists, therefore, is how predators or quasi-predators, especially such redoubtable beasts as bears and wolves, regulate their own numbers. Most prey animals are kept within bounds by being hunted—if not, they pop like popcorn until an epidemic combs through them—but what natural force rides herd on the hunters? Among bears, the burly males unquestionably pluck out and kill a proportion of the wandering young if an area becomes thick with them—as will a sow with cubs of her own kill other cubs—and the device of delayed implantation of the ova probably offers a kind of hormonal "fail-safe," by which some of the bred mothers simply do not wind up pregnant by autumn, if conditions are bad during the summer. The complexities of fertility and sterility operate as a balance wheel for wolves and mountain lions also. Several studies on these other animals are coming to fruition now, and more and more evidence points to sterility in conjunction with territoriality as the answer. To compare the findings is fascinating.

Mountain lions are geared for a life alone, and each inclines so sedulously to solitude that they rarely fight one another. The toms, in particular, according to Maurice Hornocker, don't overlap in their ranges. The females are slightly more tolerant; besides accepting some overlap among neighbors, they make adjustments of range from year to year so that those with big yearling cubs to provide for and train occupy more space than does a mother with newly born kittens. In the snowy country of central Idaho the females each have a winter range of from five to twenty square miles, and a male will encompass the home territories of two or three females, like smaller geometric figures within his own bailiwick, though he steers clear of actual contact with them except to consort briefly to breed. Mountain lions neither cooperate nor directly compete in hunting, and their scent-marking, which seems to be done mostly by the toms and which takes the form of periodically scratching with the hind feet a shovel-shaped scrape in the soil or in needles and leaves under a tree, compares with the punctilious, gossipy sort of urination male wolves indulge in and the regular round of rubbing-trees boar bears maintain. The lion is different, though, in that he doesn't pursue a rival to punish him if he is trespassing. Instead, his territoriality has been likened by Hornocker to a system of "railway signals," which, merely by notifying one cat of the presence of another, effectively "closes" that track to him. Since male mountain lions will sometimes kill kittens they come across, as boar bears kill cubs, it makes ethological sense for the species to insist upon a territoriality that is exclusive—only one dangerous male is regularly in the vicinity. On the other hand, the females, upon whom falls the responsibility of feeding the young, benefit by being willing to allow some overlap in their ranges; they can follow the game as it drifts about.

A newly grown lion setting out in its third summer from its mother's abode rambles along in an easy fashion with, in effect, a safe conduct through the territories of older lions but no desire to settle in and try to rub shoulders with them, until eventually it locates a vacant corner of the world to call its own. This impulse to clear off, which is present in young wolves and young boar bears as well, discourages inbreeding and helps to ensure that a lion lost from the population anywhere is likely to be replaced, that no plausible lion habitat goes undiscovered for long. The reclusive temperament of mountain lions befits their solitary techniques in hunting—based on the ambush, the stalk—and the way that they hunt, in turn, dovetails naturally with the abrupt, broken country they are partial to—terrain not so suited to the convivial, gang-up manner of pursuit which wolves, living usually at a lower, flatter elevation, prefer. But as is true of wolves, lions feel the urge to breed only after they have managed to establish a territory; or to put it the other way around, they do not take up permanent residence, even if they find an empty niche, until they locate scent signs and symbols around indicating that here they will be able to breed.

Despite Mech's discovery that lone wolves, dispensing with territoriality, roam more widely and often eat better than wolves in a pack, those in the prime of life do pair up and live in packs within a territorial discipline if they can. They put up an outright fighting defense once they have plumped upon ground of their own. Perhaps the fact that they fraternize so freely contributes to their readiness to fight; being sociable, they want company, but place a strict limit on how much they want. Hornocker speculates that such gregarious predators can afford the luxury of an occasional test of strength (though their howling and scent posts allay much of the need), whereas a solitary cat cannot. A mountain lion, depending wholly upon itself, must keep fit, and so as an economy measure the race has evolved a gentlefolk's way of spacing its populace about.

Individually too, bears have no other creature to lean on

except themselves, but grazing the forest meadows as they do, they can nurse an injury along when necessary, and aggressiveness toward their own kind has a biological function for them. The bullying of the weak by the strong first puts good virile genes in the cubs, then weeds out the dullards among the yearlings and two-year-olds. The ladder of dominance in a wolf pack is a matter of still greater importance, because in the relatively level country wolves frequent, where game is easier to find than in a lion's convoluted topography and where there is more of it to go around, they must have no last-minute doubts as to who is boss; they must all streak after the same beast, swarm upon it, dodge its front hooves and bring it down. The bickering and the spurting of pee on each other's piss that they like to do is not just boundary-marking, but reaffirms which one—to judge by that tangy thermostat deep inside the body (and even a dog can distinguish one unit of urine in sixty million parts of water)—will lead the charge.

Wolves and bears are fastidious in their sexual clocking, breeding only so that the bear cubs will be delivered during the denning period and the wolf puppies into the lap of the spring. If a female lion loses her kittens, however, she may come into estrus again almost immediately. She has the onerous task of killing food for the litter, as sow bears do not and a bitch wolf need not, and is more likely to lose some of them, and so is equipped for another try. But like the bear, once her young are developing, she does not breed again for two years because no pack

structure surrounds them to nurture them in the meantime. (The bitch wolf can go right at it the next February.)

Both bear and wolf scientists remark on how many of
the females they study are barren in years when, to judge
by the calendar, they ought to give birth. When an animal
requires several square miles to stretch its legs and its
psyche and to forage for food, inhibition assumes an importance. The creature must not simply be physiologically
ready for offspring; it must have a great spread of land at its
disposal, a competence, a self-confidence, and a wolf pack is
wonderfully elastic in regulating this sort of thing. The
strongest youngsters, with the wherewithal of nerve, fan
out at the age of two to colonize new territory, but the old
pack—parents, pups of the spring and yearlings of the year
before, and sometimes older shrinking violets who haven't
yet made the transition to independence, or an adopted
senior widowed wolf—continues to hold the fort.

If the hunting is good in winter it's very good, with deer
floundering in deep bogs of snow, but if it's bad, there
are no summer beaver moseying about to be ripped up
and no baby animals for hors d'oeuvres. When faced with
starvation, a pack will evaporate rapidly from eight or
ten or twelve to the single primary pair, as the others,
barred from eating the sparse kills, head away in despera-
tion to try their luck elsewhere. Then, from the odds and
ends of packs that have disintegrated, a new apportioning of the countryside occurs. Sometimes a big pack will
coalesce for a season if two former littermates, each

leader of a family on ranges that adjoin, meet affectionately again, maybe after weeks of howling to each other,
and throw in their lot together. In a pack, although several
females may be nubile, only one of them conceives, as a
rule. The lid is on unless the dominant animals are put
out of commission, whereupon all sorts of pairings become possible.

Like other recent studies (Jonkel and Cowan's in Montana, for instance), Lynn Rogers' investigations suggest
an almost equally ingenious instinctual realpolitik for
bears. No pack exists—though grizzlies occasionally are
prone to live in a loose sort of pack arrangement—but the
boar black bears of Minnesota each roam over a chunk
of geography averaging more than sixty square miles
during the June–July breeding season. This is about the
same freehold that a small wolf pack would use, but since
the bear does not need even remotely as much land for
food, he merely bestirs himself to be certain that no other
male is around where he is at the same time. Males overlap, in other words, and Rogers thinks that two miles is
about the buffer they insist upon, scratching, rubbing
against so-called bear trees for the purpose of warning
lesser males to beware. In his experience, sows seldom
make use of these signposts, but do, by contrast, appear
to enforce a severe territoriality upon each other, driving
other sows, including large ones, beyond distinct boundaries that they lay out. Although Rogers hasn't figured
out the method of marking that they employ, because the

area involved is usually less than ten square miles,* it is easier for them to exclude a trespasser than it would be for a boar to try to do the same. The boar is excellently situated, since six or eight or more sows live within his stamping grounds. Though each will be receptive to him for only a few weeks every couple of years, he doesn't have to depend on the mood and good health of any one of them in order to breed. They don't wait upon his welfare either, because each lives within the roaming range of several boars—the smaller specimens giving way before the fearsome bruisers, but skulking back. Boar bears are more likely to come to grief than sows because of their wandering disposition, yet whenever one is killed, others are on the scene—the whole uncanny setup being just the reverse of how mountain lions live.

June is an ideal month for bears to breed. They have had about three months to flesh out and recover their aplomb after the winter's sleep and plenty of opportunity remains for serious fattening before they slip below ground again. Wolves court and breed in the most grueling month instead—February, just when they should need to save their energy—but their love life goes on year-round and culminates extravagantly on the midwinter hunt. It's a time when all prudent bears are hoarding up their fat

---

* A. M. Pearson of the Canadian Wildlife Service gives a grizzly density of one bear per 10 square miles in a study area in the Yukon Territory, with the average sow's range being 27 square miles and the average boar's range 114 square miles, figures influenced by the local food supply as well as by the nature of the beasts involved.

and their newborn young under the ice and snow; the cubs grow from half a pound to five pounds before they even see the sun.

Bears hoard, wolves spend. Under the circumstances it's no wonder that scarcely half of the bitch wolves conceive, that though a wolf gives birth to at least twice as many pups as the sow does cubs, half of them probably won't survive for a year. Even the five or ten square miles the sow defends against other females would be more land than she needs for herself, if she weren't also defending nourishment for her cubs and for those of previous years. The winter of their first birthday, they den with her, then in the following summer are driven off as she keeps company with her paramours, but they are not driven outside her territory; they are still welcome there. They split up and den separately from her that fall, weighing maybe eighty pounds. In their third summer the mother appears with a new brace of cubs, and now they must keep severely clear of her. The males, not yet sexually capable, are full of urges and strike off on free-lance jaunts, as wolves and mountain lions of the same age do, each trying to light upon an empty space among the crazy quilt of bear bailiwicks that intersect throughout the forest. One young bear may travel thirty miles and set up shop, only to have a close shave with a resident bear, after which he will dash straight back to his mother's domain to recuperate for a little while before sallying forth on a different tack. Because he's slower to mature than a wolf or mountain lion, when he does find a neighborhood that suits him he has a couple of years to explore the district before committing himself. By scent he makes the acquaintance of the various sows he will pursue and the boars he must rival, eventually reaching at sexual maturity a weight of perhaps two hundred and twenty-five pounds when fat in the fall or a hundred and seventy-five pounds in the hungry spring.

Young males are the pioneers when bears resettle an area such as grown-over farmland. But they must cool their heels until a food shortage or some more arcane pressure pushes the sows toward them. Their sister cubs tend to linger in the mother's realm, living in isolation but protected from molestation by other sows because of the territorial right which they retain. One obvious effect of this procedure is that whenever a new sow does breed, her partner will probably have originated in another region, but as long as her mother remains sexually active, it appears that she will not do so. She lives there in reserve—in limbo, as it were, like an unhatched egg—in a section of her mother's territory as small as a single square mile, against the day when the elder sow meets with a disaster, whereupon the range will pass to her. Then her turf may shrink a bit, as the sows on the borders challenge her boundaries, but sooner or later she blossoms to the task of defending it.

When Rogers was starting his study, he almost ran out of funds in August when the bears he was tracking left their haunts after the agitations of the mating season, and went for trips he hadn't expected—vacations, the impulse might be called. The males sometimes travel substantial distances and mingle festively without much quarreling, and he was paying his pilot to chase them. The sows don't wander so far, but may go ten or twenty miles, as if to eat new plums and cherries, or merely ramble into an unfamiliar loop of land adjacent to their regular duchy, which for the time being they stop patrolling. This custom is another means by which bears discover gaps left by mishaps and exploit them so as to keep the countryside producing bears at full capacity. It is also a kind of relaxation which wolves could not afford because the territoriality of a wolf pack is based on the exigencies of hunting.

These are exciting discoveries, and of the several authorities engaged in zeroing in on the details, I didn't doubt that Rogers was the best. I liked his rushing way of driving and hiking and his enormous hunger for data. I liked his enthusiasm for the unfashionable black bear (there are many more scientists studying the wolf), and as we toured, enjoyed being in the shadow of a man larger and more vivid than myself—though with his bigness, as with the bigness of big women, went an affecting vulnerability. His ums and ahs annoyed me, yet I was saying um and ah myself by now. We kept remarking how we had each spent hours after school alone, daydreaming of seeing wild animals in the woods and searching out their hide-outs and handling them—not imagining that such good fortune might ever really be ours. Here we were, he said, in woods that many people drive a thousand miles to camp in, people who felt that if they could happen upon a bear it might make their whole summer excursion—and we could see one at any time.

Rogers has actually put radios on seventy-two over the years, and when he's trying to enlist somebody's support or testing a student who wants to help him, he generally goes to a den. The kids (or me, or Wally Dayton) crouch down on their hands and knees, peering into the troll-like crevice where mushrooms grow. Whether or not the smell of the bear actually persists inside, it *seems* to, and one is reminded of humble caves that a boy might run away to, and of digging to China, and of bottomless cracks in the earth. In the fall, after the bear has gone to sleep in its new hole, Rogers will tie a thread across the mouth so that on his next visit he will know whether it has woken up and scrambled outside for an interlude.

Whenever he gets near a bear in the flesh, as in mixing with them in their dens, he comes into his own—decisive, direct. Where other biologists explode the tranquilizer into an animal with a dart gun, leaving a wound, perhaps knocking the bear out of a tree so that it is killed, he does almost all his injecting by hand. The sows stand chuffing at him, slamming their paws on the ground to scare him, but he runs at them, stamping *his* feet, and stampedes both sow and cubs into separate trees. Then he climbs up and sticks the needle into their round rear ends, before lowering them one by one on a rope as the drug takes effect. Approaching a bear denned under the snow, he slips off his parka so it won't squeak as he crawls. Wriggling forward underground, he carries a flashlight in one hand and the syringe in the other, fastened to the end of a stick. If the bear is awake and panics and begins to come out, he rolls quietly to one side of the entrance and hunches there, poking it with the drug as it lumbers past; it can't get far. Sometimes bears make a blowing sound, like a man loudly cooling soup, which he listens to, not taking the warning to heart unless it is accompanied by a lifted upper lip—this being a true giveaway of belligerence. "It's like driving in town. You've got a traffic light to tell you when to stop." Usually, though, the bears stay becalmed, resting in their nests, merely sniffing the syringe when it is presented to them, making no more objection to the prick than they would to an insect's bite. He takes his time; the air inside the den is dead and hardly carries his scent.

Weather causes worse problems. Some days Rogers has to break trail on snowshoes for his snowmobile for miles, and must put the needles and vials of drugs in his mouth to warm them; the tubes of blood that he collects go in his shirt. For his blood-tapping and temperature-taking he must haul the bear outside, and if there are cubs he deals with them, squeezing into the furthest recesses but finding them unresisting once the mother has been subdued. Newborns have blue eyes and pink noses, and the smell left by his hands does not make the mother abandon them. He listens to their hearts, measures the length of their fur and wraps them in his parka until he is finished examining the mother. Even knocked out, the bears are all right in the cold, although in the summer they sometimes need to be bathed in cool water after panting in a metal trap; he washes off the matted mud if they've been struggling in a snare. After he's through, he replaces the family just as it was—wriggling inside the den, dragging the cubs and mother in after him, adjusting her posture and limbs so that she'll wake up feeling natural.

On September twenty-second we spent a red-letter day together, starting at a dump where gulls and ravens whirled above us and Rogers scanned the line of trees for any fat rear end that might be beating a retreat. He flew for four hours, locating all the bears whose radios were functioning; then back on the ground, as a check on his methods he went to three of the fixes to confirm that the bears were where he'd marked them. He inspected seven denning places, showing me how he discovers the hole itself by the raking that bears do as they collect insulation. This is while the ground is clear of snow, so he memorizes how to find it later on by lining up the nearby trees. Number 414's chamber last winter was under a clump of boulders, fifteen feet back through a passage. Number 320's was under a bulldozed pile of birch that the loggers had left. A few miles away we watched a female preparing a small basket-shaped sanctum under the upturned roots of a white pine, from which she sneaked, like a hurrying, portly child, circling downwind to identify us before clearing out. Another bear, a hundred-pound male, was hollowing a den under a crosshatch of windfalls just above a patch of swamp. He too scrambled silently away downwind ahead of us like a gentleman disturbed in a spot where he's afraid perhaps he shouldn't be.

In a pea-vine clearing Rogers photographed three bears eating and obtained some scats. He tasted bear delicacies as he walked, spitting out prickly or bitter leaves. In one of his traps was a young male, chopping its teeth, clicking its tongue, with a strong ursine smell of urine. Rogers answered with the same sounds, and when he let the bear loose it bounded toward the woods like the beast of a children's fairy tale—a big rolling derrière, a big tongue for eating, and pounding feet, its body bending like a boomerang

We ate rock tripe off the rocks, saw moose tracks, wolf scats, two red-tailed hawks, three deer and a painted turtle. The dogwood was turning purple now, the aspens golden, the plum bushes red, the pin cherries brown, and the birches and hazel and thimbleberries yellow. There was pearly everlasting, and blue large-leafed aster still blooming in the woods, and sweet fern that we crushed in our hands to smell. Alders had grown up higher than the jeep on some of the roads we followed. "Doesn't have too much traffic," said Rogers.

There is sometimes a sadness to David Mech's work, when he knows in advance from the blood tests he does which of his wolf pups is going to die. But Rogers' cubs are hardier, the winter hold no terrors for them, and when they do disappear it is not due to the sort of anemia which an investigator can foresee. I thought very highly of him—this admirable animal-catcher, this student of wild foods and smells, this scholar of garbage dumps. Because his bears like dumps, so does he.

APOCALYPSE
ENOUGH:
OF NEWTS
AND MICE

Remember back when people carried a rabbit's foot and called avocados "alligator pears," when "a mile a minute" was traveling fast, and crime meant only Frank Costello? Remember squiring Lucy to the soda fountain: this years before anybody could hope to "get in her pants"? Nevertheless, we knew as we watched her licking vanilla from a long-handled spoon that to provide such fare was a form of possession— down went the blobby mouthfuls. Already we had some sense that sex itself must be a feast, or if not that, at least a meal. At any age it still is an intimate business to furnish food to a woman, or to be cooked for by her, like lying next to each other for a little.

That was the era when the boy, growing into a man,

could "wreck" a girl if he got her into trouble and didn't marry her. Later, if he'd done right by her, she had her own capricious moment of reckoning up accounts. If she chose to divorce him she could "take him to the cleaners"; and people gorged on such decisions, lunching with lawyers, brooding with buddies. But as we looked ahead, the shortened work week, advancing educational levels, were going to lead to all manner of elegant self-cultivation and comradely comity, and on the other hand, to 3-D TV "feelies" for the evening hours: what a star system that would promote! It was going to be marvelous—the new architecture working wonders with space, and old age a period of repletion, so that life's fullness would be prolonged.

Now each year we are flush up against the possibility that ten million people or more will starve, instead. Starvation isn't new, but it is unprecedented that people ten thousand miles away should have such foreknowledge and have to decide what to do. Friends and figures I admire speak of these years as apocalyptic, and if the word, as in the dictionary, refers to revelations of "splendor, magnitude . . . hiddenness of meaning," that might not be so bad, but their tone usually denotes cataclysm. Though we'd got used to witnessing on television not only mad bombings at home but in every other part of the world (our modern fascination with psychology helped and we believed it was part of the diversity to come), to learn that our innocent taste for sirloin is linked to starvation is a burden that is new. Think how painful in a decade or so the recent starvation south of the Sahara would have seemed. No mere random drought: the rain-makers could have diverted rainfall from Arkansas's corn-fields and Russia's wheat. You are overpopulated, the Russo-American rainmakers would claim. We are starving, the Africans would say, as all of us simultaneously watched on the home screen. And if we then kept those scenes off the screen, it would be a paralyzing setback, because the premise of this civilization has been that human life is precious, even more so as we have jettisoned the idea of God as a force to blame or to cushion the chill, including therefore in our calculations the democratic poor and sick.

All but a garden-variety nature was sacrificed too when we started outfitting ourselves for the democratic future that we were sure was in store. The one principle we did stick to was the notion that human life—each human life—was irreplaceable; and so it hurts, it's bewildering, to consider that human nature may not be precious to us either, after all. Already it is harder to be civilized when every manifestation of misery in the world is visually at hand, as we so choose. And we must choose, we've burned our bridges, and if we're now forced to conclude that human life does *not* count, walling ourselves away from the starving (no war going on to excuse us), we will have no beliefs to fall back on—not God, nature or democracy. Not family either, since the first fallout of technology has vitiated the family as a stronghold.

Even in the fatter countries cheeseparing has become the rule; the expansive wonders that were spoken of, like nuclear power, have proven problematic, disappointing.

But this deterioration in living conditions should not seem surprising. The remarkable thing to me has always been how few people are killed in accidents or murdered or die of pneumonia before their time. The heap of neatly butchered beef spread on the counter, the deep-sea fish of exuberant variety, have been equally extraordinary, and so to learn that the fish are running out, and beef becoming an ambiguous luxury, is scarcely a surprise. The aim of medical science remains, as always, to "defeat" death, yet if this effort should somehow be crowned with success, jelled just as we are, with the same pop singers, opinion leaders, public athletes—Barbra Streisand, Teddy White, Muhammad Ali—we would soon die of boredom and exasperation.

Yet how tough we are: those jungle Japanese who hold out thirty years alone on an island, just as a holocaust survivor might, and longer than Ishi, the last wild Indian in America, was able to. And how adaptable: the idea that women will soon play full-fledged roles in the world, that one will be dealing with them everywhere, not only in the evenings and on weekends, as alarming as it seemed to many of us who were unprepared for it, is just the sort of development to prove that the boundaries of how we live are opening outward at the same time as in other ways they appear to be closing fast. Locally, along comes Women's Liberation, and none too soon, because as life in general becomes more communal and regimented, we're speeding toward a time when there won't be much space for masculine aggressiveness of any kind, and "women," at least as we've visualized them, may be better suited to

73

practicing practically any profession than "men."

That women have decided to make more of a show in the world exactly when men are feeling so frayed produces a little heartburn all around, and one of the current puzzles is whether women, as they obtain performers' positions, will be able to uproot their previous insistence upon the talismans of success in a lover, rather than supportive qualities. There are men around to fill the bill, but will they continue to rebuff them, coveting the fellow with the feather in his cap, a breadwinner, a Zapata? As is so frequent in these futuristic collisions, the upshot may be only a redisposal, a different use for separate men. This would be the sort of outcome nature delights in. Man on top, man on the bottom, woman between, or vice versa: serial, interrupted, incomplete alliances.

However, with fewer children to be had, the childbearing years will come to seem as privileged and nostalgia-washed as the collegiate stint of Dink Stover: none of this idea that one should plunk the tot in a day-care center. On the contrary, a career will be more commonplace than having children. With all the troubles lying in store—not just cramped backs and anorexia and rectal cancer and highway crime and kinky religion (even our dogs are experiencing an epidemic of epilepsy), but murder clubs and spates of suicide—rearing children will be seen as a sanctuary. Indeed, a woman's veto on the matter will give her enough leverage for one last victory in the war of the sexes.

As always, sex will succor us, except that in manipulating the orgasm, we will perhaps suddenly take notice of it with a sense of panic. Sex and romantic love are primeval compulsions that point toward giving birth, and we couldn't do without them; they have never been more necessary, but for a novel reason—psychic, not primarily biological survival now—toward which purpose we toy with them and soup them up, interrupt, repeat the fling, turn it bottomside up, abort the conclusion, like feasters who tickle their tonsils after each large helping in order to start all over again. So because the source of all this efflorescence is becoming fossilized, and because tinkering with fossilized instincts is going to bring on vertigo—a griping sensation, a kind of menopause, then apathy—although there is no set inventory of love and sex to run out of, at first we'll feel that we've run out.

Of course the sweetest healing still occurs in that old breeding position that we love so much even when we don't intend to breed. Adventurers stock up on sex like camels, then go without, vociferously grumbling, which we quite like them for; we are amused. Ascetics regard it even more solemnly, forgoing it as if it were such powerful medicine that the hunger alone is an elixir. Just as with food, one cannot actually abstain from sex or love. Confined in solitude, you'll eat your boots, you'll grow fond of the bugs that cross the floor.

Sex started so simply. Mum fed us milk of her own creation, after accommodating us within herself, yet Dad was stronger and more penetrating than Mum. By now we've improvised as many codas on this as would be possible with all the chords of music, but because sex is not an art but a hunger, we are in danger of flattening the varia-

75

tions to a monotone when distracted by other interests. The swing to unisex anticipates this—neutral colorations, nobody rocking the boat. Running against it, inevitably, is still the breeze of flirtation, because nearly everybody who wants to be businesslike also wishes to be in love. There is the sense that one must seize the day, the short daylight is waning, and if one cannot have a love affair one isn't living. Life always was considered to be love—love of God and the kids—but people want the freshest sensation, to be *in* love, and will insist upon it, and so from flirtation, infatuation and love—here we go again—eventually evolves marriage, self-sacrifice, a performer and a helper, and loneliness for the outsider.

Apocalypse enough, to be aware of living upon borrowed time. Imagine talking with a seaman in the long epoch of sailing ships, a man who worked with the slant of the wind against a mast. Telling him, no, there weren't going to be any more ships that sailed, only container ships with a twelve-hour turnaround in port, whose seamen mostly scraped paint. Or telling a frontiersman, with his long legs, no more gold strikes to look for, no more traplines that might encompass an entire river system. "How's a man like me going to live?" the fellow would exclaim—just as we do sometimes. But in talking with him, we'd smile, knowing that the world has really grown bigger, and not smaller, since his day, more varied and intriguing —or that in any case the rest of us have been so altered in keeping pace with it that we would be devastated if the clock were actually turned back.

Of course it's safer to take a calm view of what's ahead,

because if the sky falls in nobody is going to bother looking around for the optimist to sneer at him. There is always a split vision when one looks at people, as if first the right eye were blocked off, and then the left. Momentarily, one despairs that these individuals, either apart or together, will ever manage even to begin to direct their affairs, much less do more than just go through the motions. But half an hour later one is marveling instead at the texture of qualities complementing and reinforcing each other. What will constitute excellence in a nation already industrialized? Will it be recycling technology, land-use planning, the upgrading of the poor and sick? A greenhouselike protection of originality in the sciences and arts while all the other old, wild and woolly outflashings of the spirit are tamped down? If so, there will be a lot of roaming, until at last the continents have come to fully resemble one another—and then where will the energetic go?

Maybe they won't go anywhere, just as nobody nowadays would really want to hike nine hundred miles in muck and snow to trap beaver. Never yet has a societal revolution developed of itself so quickly that the people concerned didn't divine what was happening and dash around in front. An old man reflecting on the pleasures he enjoyed that are no longer available would think, *What they don't know won't hurt them.* On the other hand, these are also the sentiments of those who look at *him.* Naturally we will attempt to garden in the realm of human nature, not for the first time but of necessity more single-mindedly, there being no longer other realms. And alongside the agony of starvation will be the question of starvation. Self-abnegation, self-immolation: instead of crew-cut versus long-haired Americans, it will be the plump and thin. The conduct of the Catholic Church of Paul VI will be scanned as critically as Pius XII's has been. If need be, we will study death.

But a woman doesn't lose her beauty in a year, nor a man his strength; the stages of deterioration proceed as a muddy feeling in the muscles or a change that shows after a bath when the hair sticks against the skull, with the face white. Neither should an apocalypse strike too precipitately, if there is to be one. We can be sure that a resurgence of religious patience and faith will accompany the starving time, just as it is already arranged that the strength of women is the weakness of men.

My own best premonition of life is of a rhythm like that of dolphins. Water, air, water, air—to soothe the skin, then feed the lungs. Coasting in one medium, then down into another, and up briefly sailing again. Not too complicated a cadenza—in fact, less complicated than the conditions—but gay enough and not destructive of ancestral pleasures. Soldiers are lonesome now that nobody idealizes war, and many housewives are scrambling in confusion for a second career; yet if you take the trouble to look through the papers of any family which still keeps papers, up in that leather trunk in the dust of the attic, what you will find is packets of a soldier's letters from Fort Rice in the Dakota Territory to his wife in Philadelphia. One needn't advocate wars for men and domesticity for women to point out the difficulty of managing a balancing act between the pleasure the two sexes draw from each other because they are so different and the pleasure of working with members of the opposite sex as if they weren't all that different.

What is most shocking is not how casually we accept the news of an acquaintance's death unless our noses are rubbed in it, but how casually we observed his *life*. We simply speculate, take note and watch. How does he look this year: below par, chapfallen, drinking? We glance at what he's up to as at a game that he is playing and losing, while trying fitfully to reconstruct our own—if this was *it*, how we would moan. When they sum up, old men often will claim that their children mattered most to them; the middle-aged may say that it is the act of love. (In keeping with this temptation to speak of what one either has already had or must wait for, younger men mention their careers.) But one reason why we have children is that we remember being mothered and fathered and can slip back again through them to participate in the embrace. Bestowing it, we stamp them with the embrace they will seek.

A friend of mine woke up to how short life is when he was driving in California with a bunch of chums. The talk had not been cheerful; the driver, a stranger to him, was depressed. "I'll see you all in Hell!" the driver said abruptly, swerving the car against a cliff, where everybody died except my friend.

Another friend, at eighty-some, is setting off this fall on what he describes as his last trip. He's going back to Alberta, where he homesteaded along the Swan River fifty years ago. Afterwards he raised a family in New England; otherwise he might not be so serene about the finality of this lark. He sells night crawlers and root beer from a stand next to the highway, but has a panorama of people and events to contemplate.

That's what we want—love and scenery behind us to look back on. That we should be able to move about reasonably freely in the meantime without regard to roles is not debatable. The dolphin, living vertically, has it both ways—in winter, the cold wind and warm water, in the summer the cold water and warm wind. And what *we* have, besides our quicksilver unisex scene, is the past to dive into—old salve for new dilemmas. The past is, among other things, hunter-gatherer and mother, a possibility we will want to retain, men as men, women as women, juggling our animosities alongside the intimacy of conjugality, brothers, sisters, colleagues, lovers.

I live half the year by kerosene, and go into the woods with a dog and goat trotting ahead, the goat browsing on wintergreen and sumac, basswood and serviceberry leaves, while the dog quarters for game—a hunter and a nibbler, like the twin horns of the animal kingdom. My friend who homesteaded on the Swan River spent so much time in that sanguine country that even in hardscrabble Vermont, when gazing at the ledge of granite across the lake from him, he'll say he'd bet he would find gold there if he had the money to blast for it. Because his spring water has iron in it that stains his cup, he's also sure there's a potential iron mine on the mountain behind his house; if he was rich he'd buy the slope and wrench it out. He says his lake has fish to scare a man. (In mine, he claims they'd eat a man.) His wife got hold of some money and bought a Cadillac, and he began building a garage for it on the lake bank, but before he finished she left in the Cadillac. What he does know about is his lake—the 40-foot-deep shelves, and where drowned swimmers lie, and where the fishes feed—so when he sizes up a tourist while renting a boat to him, he can determine just about how many bass or togue the fellow catches by where he points and the advice he gives. With frontier prodigality, he himself is likely to fish the spawning beds, where the best cocks and hens will hook themselves while angrily rooting his bait away from their nests. He hunts with a boy's small .22, so that the only deer that hears him shoot will be the deer he kills. He is an optimist of the stripe that may be said to have made this country great and seems to be dying out, though there are other optimists about.

A beaming farmer of the middle class, a convert to the Jesus Movement, dropped in on me one evening to persuade me to volunteer for Christ. There are local people, too, who somehow in Bolivia's altitudes learned to, as they say, align their "stomachs, hearts and heads." What is really happening, however, is ubiquitous and not to be dismissed. We have learned to sniff each other, as ants do, in haste, taking for granted with the sniff that we know all about the person. Around the old-time bar or barber shop there always were code words that served the same purpose, but these are much reduced. We assume we know what someone means as soon as he starts, because, first of all, we hardly care—we can write off any number of people and there will still be plenty more—and, secondly, so few distinctions of region or class remain that in moving about, with a few sniffs, we think we can pick up right where we left off in another portion of the herd. And this is a profound change.

Among the several communes hereabouts is one especially known for its turnover: sometimes new faces every week. When they succeed, communes are an exaggeration of friendly fellowship, and when they don't, of disconnectedness; they are a laboratory of leaders and followers, and no less interesting now that their star among young people has waned. As a movement, they began as another attempt to fling away the galling feeling so many people have of living in the world only to eat—the socalled rat race—instead of eating in order to live. They failed at least partly because the enormous amounts of time consumed in raising food—the quasi-mystical emphasis upon home-grown food—wound up as just another version of living in order to eat. Nevertheless, some groups get by amiably year after year, pooling their houses, gardens, cars, with little more than a Sunday sauna or wine party as a ceremonial. But this particular commune of the Open Door tries to cement everybody tightly with a supper each night around a big table, all twenty of them silently clasping hands beforehand in what they are pleased to call grace, with the Aladdin lamp turned low. Some are groggy, rickety specimens, casualties of the age, and squeeze one's hands until one must squeeze back in self-defense. Maybe my hunger, too, as I wait through the silence for my bowl of tomatoes and chard increases my uneasiness. The water jar is shared; even the dental-flossing after the meal is all but communal. As a rule, these aren't people of many words, and so one doesn't have the chance to look into their faces that ordinarily comes with conversation. Instead, I wonder how they will weather the ensuing months and what has happened to the collection of crash transients whose hands I clasped tightly last year.

The ceremony of grace being promulgated presumes, of course, brotherhood as a religion; yet the spaces around the table from month to month are filled interchangeably. I don't say that the idea of brotherhood and interchangeability is contradictory. Quite the opposite; without God, without nature, and ourselves cheek by jowl, we are being forced into it by our religious impulse. It seems to be the wave of the future, even in our Western democracies, and this is what is apocalyptic and alarming.

Once, in the biology lab at boarding school, I discovered a terrarium that had been forgotten about for several weeks. The moss had died, the soil had cracked, the pool of water had shrunk to scum. Among the creatures which had existed there only a few newts had survived, and these were tottering skeletons, barely alive. Two lay dead, partially devoured; there had been more. But one newt was a brazen exception. Red, vigorous, spruce as a bugler, tall as a tiger, he broadcast good health and exultancy. He hadn't simply outlasted the ordeal; he stood up on his toes and practically crowed.

Once, too, I saw a cannibal mouse—a laboratory mouse, cannibal not from necessity but out of verve (or so it seemed). He was horrible; he was manic—in fact a maniac—but he was vital, undeniably, and looked just like the sort of gleeful madman who comes trudging off a snowfield and gets his photograph taken with a beard grown even bushier because of his ordeal. So it is likely to be with some of the survivors of the disasters forecast for the coming years. They will be manic, too, and vital, if one leaves out the possibility of catastrophes of the sort in which their body chemistry would have changed. After walking through a landscape of famine they won't be the same as you and me, but they will have children who will be human beings.

HEROES

AND

FOOTFALLS

At Yankee Stadium thirty years ago we'd crowd down to the front of the grandstand as the game worked to a close, hunching so the people sitting there would not complain to an usher. The ushers' job was to keep the field clear until the final out, but as the ball was caught, their resistance turned to remonstrance, as if to say you *shouldn't*. We scrambled across the barriers, hundreds of us, to intercept the players running for the dugout, running to the brink of it ourselves, seeing their graceful stoop for the low roof. In their white uniforms Joe DiMaggio and Snuffy Stirnweiss, Charlie Keller, Phil Rizzuto, all looked marvelously tall and seemed to personify the very prime of life and what it could embody in effectiveness. They ran in loping strides, not ragged bursts, like us, and though we ran right next to them, most of us didn't try to touch them and hardly dared to call their names. Half of the excitement was also just being on the playing field, so green in the colossal stadium. Many people felt the same, streaming in leisurely fashion onto the diamond, strolling slowly toward the bleacher exits and turning to look back because, besides a parklike setting, it was grass on which extraordinary men had done fine deeds.

Johnny Mize switched over from the National League to play first base in the twilight of his career, and there were visitors like Hank Greenberg in the traveling team's gray uniform to admire occasionally, along with New York's own roster of pitchers, each one taking his turn, but the build-up of years of radio listening was what mattered in our worship of those several more familiar figures. We saw them only three or four times in a season, when we spent the money for a ticket, but the radio (or for our fathers, maybe the sports page) served up a clarified profile of an athlete we could look up to. No bleary succession of games televised daily, no muzzy appearance on *Laugh-In* to confuse us, no chuckling debut on the *Merv Griffin Show* to blur the tall image: instead, simply "Joltin' Joe," or "Scooter," or "Old Reliable."

To be next to DiMaggio was most exciting and undoubtedly he was the one I loved, but just as in school I hung around the *second*-prettiest girl, so Tommy Henrich, of the 1948 Yankees, was my particular hero. He was a clutch player whose averages in the record book give no indication of how well he could play in the last innings of a close game. He concentrated his ability and played like DiMaggio whenever it counted, and since I suspected that I was not destined to be a DiMaggio myself, he delighted me.

Today nobody is permitted on the field to touch the

players after a game—this partly to save the grass but also to protect the players. We kill our heroes nowadays; as too much admiration fixes upon them, a killer emerges, representing more than just himself. The impact of the first Kennedy assassination, confirmed by later deaths and shootings, cannot be overestimated. Afraid of what will happen if we admire somebody too much, we look a little to one side, take care to hedge our praise until, like other feelings that go unsaid too long, it loses immediacy. The very character of admiration has changed.

Even leaving out the factor of celebrity, in any running big-city crowd there is likely to be a man with a knife now anyway, and many of us, without carrying knives, have been discovering our own startling capacity for vengeance. Month after month, it's been a case of sitting back and watching a Vice President and President weaken, wither, whiten, age and crack before our eyes, a process most of us have watched implacably, and not just those who disliked the power and policies of these two men from the beginning. It's a destructive time. People with a historical imagination (and grateful for small entertainments) could bake up from the biscuit mix of the 1960s a simulated private theater of civil war: misery, disorders, citizens voting by the length of their hair, and so forth. Lately, without laboring at it, they can apprehend what a monarchy was like when an unwanted king was on the throne, regarded as unfit and crippled, without popular backing, yet with the country's fortunes in his fingers. Life in America, a nation of believers, has gone drab and Eastern European (as we used to picture Eastern Europe) while we wait for the inventions to materialize that will define the way we're going to live.

Such a climate is splendid for the ironists, the intellectuals, the spiritually self-sufficient, the self-employed. Before, our way of living gradually evolved from discoveries like the use of electricity and oil, but having overshot all that, we hang suspended, anticipating that technology is going to catch up finally and put a flooring under us. When the engineers, agriculturists and government inflation experts have so failed in their predictions, we don't idealize them. Naturally, too, when most Americans regard themselves as middle-class, physicians are noticed now as much for profiteering as for their learned opinions and selfless house calls. And when the Vietnam war went sour, not only did the glamour of soldiers and sailors evaporate, but also that of the astronauts, because the government had insisted upon running the space program like a B-52 mission—politically linked to the war, indeed. They were guinea pigs—chewed out if they so much as carried a corned-beef sandwich along—and a far cry from the great, raunchy, individualist explorers like Hernando Cortez.

President Nixon's fatherly simper when he makes a speech, his playful roll of the shoulders that must hark back to some wistful memory of football and that chimed in with some gauche insecurity in many voters to win for him, have curdled to a ghostly joke. After the scandals he is dying on the vine, and now the low-grade infection is systemwide. In the cat's cradle of Watergate, Elliot Richardson has been too ambiguous and Sam Ervin too rehearsed. In Congress, the conservatives are not up to the mark: thus the prominence of William Buckley. Neither have the liberals: thus Ralph Nader. But Buckley has been essentially only a witty debater with a winning collegiate smile, popping eyes and bloody mind; and Nader is a raider, not a builder, not acceptably mainstream.

To explain the obvious—why experts and physicians, soldiers and public servants aren't heroes to anyone right now—doesn't account for the absence of other heroes, however. You'd think a nutty buccaneer like Howard Hughes would attract a following in parlous times: the billionaire with no pleasures, afraid to look at people, yet not a mingy fellow like J. Paul Getty. Unfortunately the anti-hero shot his bolt as a folk figure some time ago, even the classy existential variety. Existentialism, like a stock broker, has been "discounting" the future all along, until now that the future is here, existentialism itself has been discounted. We're sick of all the anti-heroes—"Wild Ones" on a motorcycle, and the rest of them—and yet don't throb for a traditional figure, such as Cesar Chavez, either. Chavez represents the sweat of the brow, which is not what we care about right now, and whereas our reaction to Howard Hughes makes no practical difference, in the case of Chavez, along with denying him our adulation, we probably foreclose his chances of real success as well.

Henry Kissinger is traditional hero material, like Chavez, except that we seem to know too much history, chatting casually of Metternich, Bismarck and Talleyrand, and could believe him to be the best foreign secretary in living memory without being roused to any pitch of enthusiasm. His own self-deprecating fatalism, which would have stigmatized him as a comic refugee a decade or more ago, complements this, nicely contemporary. Heroism is in the eye of the beholder: we have no tolerance now. Some unfashionable piece of eccentricity or minor bit of insight—that Kissinger is "compensating," or Daniel Berrigan courts martyrdom, or Bobby Fischer is a little creepy—short-circuits our normal impulse to admire the out-of-the-ordinary. We have no forbearance. Besides, the times are upside down, so that Berrigan, whose heroism ought properly to lose, is confounded to find that he wins, and Kissinger, whose every exertion has been to win since he first sought to connect himself to Nelson Rockefeller, discovers himself inch by inch constrained to lose. So instead nostalgia intrigues us, because the dead come neatly packaged, with nothing veering out of character to surprise us—or if we do alter the received opinion of a heroic personality like T. E. Lawrence, we seem ready to reinterpret all the data just as simplistically as his comrades viewed it.

Although this has been among the richest periods in popular entertainment, the stars flip in and out of the limelight almost too fast to register, each famous for about fifteen minutes. In the arts, apparently it's one of those disappointing intervals when the creative people aren't quite as good as the performers. At the best of times the arts do get a little fusty—white-haired personages locking up their papers for the next fifty years in a last will and testament, as if anybody could be sure that there will *be* another fifty years. Nevertheless, with artists around like

Robert Motherwell and Thornton Wilder, you'd think we'd make more of a fuss. Even intellectuals like Albert Schweitzer or Albert Einstein would get short shrift, the one because the agnosticism of the age would roll over his philanthropy, the other because we'd dread the results of his scientific discoveries. Only a persecuted Russian novelist might fill the bill, or someone else both foreign and political, on the order of Pablo Casals. (Though we do like our artists to be political, Ezra Pound was not quite foreign enough to escape being pilloried by the familiar Soviet tactic with enemies of the state: confinement in a lunatic asylum for many years.)

Henry James wrote a short story called "The Real Thing," in which a painter looks for an aristocratic couple to model for him and finds that though two actual aristocrats hard-pressed for funds are indeed willing to pose, they can't seem to convey the reality he seeks as well as a pair of scruffy gypsies do. Any journalist can attest to a similar discovery. If for some reason he wants to interview the man who has accomplished the best original work in a particular field, not just the famous popularizer who appears in public frequently, he may have to travel a bit, meeting with idiosyncrasy, but when he does make contact the man's schedule will not be such as to require excessive juggling; in fact the fellow may be as poor as a church mouse and have nobody else to talk to. It isn't only that "recognition" has been delayed, but that the attributes that carried the day for him are not necessarily magnetic or even personable. Nobody has been seeking him out, because he isn't fun to interview.

It's not as if we don't need heroes, however. They dramatize solutions and help to pave the way through new circumstances; they stumble on a stance that suits nearly everybody. The trouble is, we have so much bitterness to put behind us that we laugh at all solutions. On Vietnam, the doves did in the hawks and the hawks the doves, so that, for skepticism, the effects of that disaster, like the assassinations, won't soon stop reverberating. Heroes embody aspirations that we ourselves share, or remember fondly, and to be cored of heroes is to be cored of aspirations; it is unusual to begrudge honest achievement its due.

Not many years have passed since the first tuba notes of self-deflation sounded after the victories of World War II. Down in Texas, where the custom was to label merchandise as "Made in Texas by Texans," several Volkswagen drivers glued on a coy black bumper sticker: "Made by der Elves in der Black Forest." This had a sympathetic flavor, and we went on to the era of the individual versus the regime. Yet though on the one hand we had perhaps once been too regimented to agree wholeheartedly upon a hero, on the other, we were not now quite polarized enough: there was no real regime. Angela Davis was acquitted. The Chicago Seven are not in jail. The Bomb was never dropped over North Vietnam. Whatever one may have thought of Haldeman and Ehrlichman, nobody who has ventured west of Hoboken can seriously suppose that we were ever in danger of a workable *Putsch*.

America is irrevocably a democracy, and the mood upon us at the moment is that we know almost everything, have digested the principal revelations and encountered the disillusions, so that whatever surprises lie in store will amount to more of the same. We feel as if we know more than we want to know on almost any subject, that what counts is still that same sore kernel of sensibility—being lonesome, finding sex is too much for us, and that we have no firm predictions to make, personally or nationally, except to believe that just as nothing is permanent, neither is anything temporary.

So much of the new is old. A recent issue of *Rolling Stone*, a new-wave publication, featured Richard Goodwin's New Frontier moralisms heisted West from the Kennedy compound; and then an article about life in the (in this case) Playboy Mansion; and then another about Alcatraz, just like *The Police Gazette* of forty years ago. Those are our bedrock imaginings: Ourselves Imprisoned and Ourselves Free. The Fortas-Agnew-Nixon type of fall-of-the-mighty we can take in stride because corruption is an ancient spectacle, at worst startling, like a suicide. The Great Depression of the thirties did scar and scare people, however, like the assassinations lately, as if a fault had opened in the earth. The "nuclear capability," as it is ingeniously called, again tipped everybody toward unthinkable eventualities, and now the recent technological miscues, such as the "energy crisis," that follow one upon another faster and faster, continue to unsettle us, where wiring that we knew nothing about has gone askew.

These seem to be footfalls of enormous changes to come, although, being numb, we don't believe in them; nostalgia absorbs whatever spirit of enthusiasm might otherwise single out a hero to lead the way. Society has

become too classless, with no elite, no anti-elite, too swift
a patter of communication, not enough anger or excitement, innocence or mystery. The sights from an airplane,
even above a mat of cloud cover, are themselves worth the
fare, and yet most of us scarcely look; and piloting has not
caught on—it used to be assumed that kids would be fiddling around the county airport just as they fooled with
jalopies. Instead, everybody is taking up tennis or skiing,
or other statusy hush-puppy avocations that keep the
mouth too full to squawk. People have to hate the rich a
bit to recognize a Robin Hood or Roosevelt. The Greeks,
in order to burnish Achilles to a golden hue, needed their
slaves to boot around, much as we needed our Negroes to
give Abraham Lincoln a backdrop. (Schweitzer's blacks,
of course, were *sick*.) Contrast is the key to it. Inherent in
hero worship is a brutality—the drinking poet, the rock
star autographing his groupies' breasts. After all, there is
no President that Billy Graham and Sammy Davis Jr.
would not have hugged.

We have nobody any more who really grins—no Ike.
Grinning itself went out of style with Mad Magazine's
Alfred E. Neuman. And the way we tend to quickly quit
our marriages now thickens the climate for disillusion,
temporizing and the other qualities that are opposed to
idolizing a hero, who above all must be committed. Hector
was a hero on behalf of family, dying for his home and
Troy. Achilles was a hero on behalf of man himself—man
exercising a great gift for the sake of fame, man at his
exuberant prime and at a kind of summit. Achilles out-
shines Hector for us because exuberance and fame and

life lived at a pitch are what we still dream of. But Odysseus was a hero at simply surviving—eating, swimming—on finally no one's behalf but his own, not even for *machismo*, which explains why he, the best of all, has stood the test of time.

Yet, like agnosticism or anything else that rubs away the traditional demarcations, the new vogue of unisex is bad for heroism on the whole. And though it is a question whether the appeal of Ted Williams' idiosyncrasies would have survived television, a bigger obstacle for him or for any other hero would be not so much television as the people who are watching it. We lack patience nowadays—one slip and we will damn somebody. And we're not yet at home with all our pop psychological theories about hard work, ambition, courage and selflessness; they too undercut our appreciation. One must love one's heroes, notwithstanding their pains, self-doubts, boring inconsistencies, and this is much more difficult with overexposure. Also, perhaps we're too bewildered; before we can forgive them, we must forgive ourselves. After the present scandals and crises have been resolved, the first ticker-tape parade we hold should be for us.

A RUN
OF
BAD LUCK

Bad ions in the air, bad stars, or bad luck: call it what you will—a run of bad luck, in fact. I was driving down the Thruway in Vermont to consult a doctor in New York, and hit a deer. Didn't see the deer till the impact, sharing its surprise. Deer, unlike domestic animals, are afraid of cars and leap as you pass, either into you or away. It lay in the deep grass, heaving like a creature stranded on the beach.

Sure enough, as befitted the omen, in New York City the doctor's news was bad. Then within a day or two, Pier 50, a huge ramshackle structure across the street from where I live, caught fire and burned hectically for seven hours, although surrounded by fireboats, as only an abandoned pier can. The neighborhood was layered in smoke for a couple of days—for me, acrid testimony to what the doctor had said. There were also a few of the usual New York hang-up phone calls, and then, as if to push me into a sump of depression, somebody—a vandal aroused by the fire, or someone who thought I had parked in his parking space—

poured sugar into the gas tank of my car, not enough to destroy the engine but enough so that I returned to Vermont in relief.

In the meantime, my mother, in another city, had gone into the hospital for surgery, and one evening that week my daughter and I were out walking along a wooded road (I was carrying her on my shoulders), when a car passing another car bore down on us at high speed, its roar not easy to distinguish from that of the slower one; I barely heard it in time. This, in the context of the other incidents, particularly shook me because it seemed to bear a hint of malevolence; I felt very small. Then, within days, my next-door neighbor there, an old man as close as a relative to us, died of a stroke. Another good friend and country mentor went into the hospital after a heart attack. News came from New York as well that a friend in the city had killed herself. I marshaled a motley assortment of tranquilizers and sleeping pills left over from the past— divorce, career crisis, other bad occasions. I had that feeling of luck running out, that I must be *very careful*, although, on the contrary, I was becoming deadened, not alert. At such a time, the opposite of invulnerable, one must take care to move in a gingerly fashion and not get so rattled that an accident happens. I had considered myself a sort of a Sunday's child much of my life, but suddenly intimations of death and calamity were all about.

I remembered talking to a woman who had survived a snowslide by swimming along on the surface while whooshing downhill for a hundred yards—as people caught in an undertow or even in quicksand save themselves by flattening out and floating if they can. Just so, I should ride the current until it turned. The best advice I have heard on bearing pain is to fix one's mind upon the idea that the pain is in one place—the other side of the room—and that you are in another; then, where you are, play cards or whatever. Cooking, fooling with my daughter, I realized more distinctly than at any time in years that although in fact my life was not at stake right now, I believed in some form of reincarnation or immortality—this a conviction, not a wish. I pray in airplanes during takeoff, but it is with a sense of praying *pro forma*, as if the location of my belief weren't really there, but were more generalized, in a bigger God. There are ideas central to society which we seldom question in order that society will hold together— as, for instance, the notion basic to medical care that everybody has a contribution to make, or "a right to life." But there are other conceptions, such as the idea of God, which we disparage and scarcely consider, until later, smiling sheepishly in our mind's eye as if we had disputed the fact that the moon moves in the sky, we admit to having been wrong, and to having known all along that we were wrong.

Once, highborn ladies would flee to a convent if some unnerving sequence of events overtook them, not necessarily taking orders, but resting, collecting their wits. And when they strolled in the cloister around a bubbling fountain, the walkway itself possessed a soothing, perpetual quality, with each right-angle turn leading straight to another. Walking for many hours, they looked at the linden-wood saints, the robust faces—at the Virgin's implacable verve, or else at a dolor portrayed with an equally saving exaggeration. Coincidentally, I went to New York's own Cloisters, and because the reality of each bad event had been dulled by the others, it was for me one of those queer times when people recognize how much they can adjust to —how quickly, for example, they could settle into the routine of life in a prison camp.

Of course I had my daughter to entertain, and in the country I walked in the woods, watching the aspens quake (said by legend to occur because Christ's cross was of aspen). I have an old army siren, hand-cranked, that I climbed with up on the mountain at twilight, to persuade a family of coyotes nearby to answer. I was relieved that the random incidents seemed to have ended. I thought of two friends in the city who had recently suffered crises— heart attacks at forty. One fellow, as the pain surged through him, found himself muttering stubbornly, "No groveling, Death!" When he was out of danger he wrote seventy-some letters to friends from his hospital bed, each with a numbered series of thoughts directed to the recipient. The other man is that rare case where one can put one's finger exactly on the characteristics of which one is so fond. He married the same woman twice. Although it didn't work out either time, she was well worth marrying twice, and to my way of thinking this showed that he was at once a man of fervent, rash, abiding love, and yet a man of flexibility, ready to admit an error and to act to correct it.

Both my mother and country mentor were now on the mend, and my own doctor reported good news. Prospects began looking up. What I'd gained from the period, besides a flood of relief, was the memory of how certain I'd been that the intricacy and brilliance of life cannot simply fold up with one's death—that, as in the metaphor of a fountain, or the great paradigm of rain and the ocean, it sinks down but comes up, blooms up and sinks down again.

PATHOS

AND

PERFECTION

We who go to the circus every year should explain that we go *expecting* to see the same feats performed all over again. The circus is composed of familiar acts that we know by heart and that mesh together, rather like the episodes in an epic poem. As might have befitted Homer's era, a troupe of wanderers comes to town, each man recites a wonderful piece we already knew all about, there is heroism, dedication, and the brilliance lies in the way it's all put together.

Jugglers stamp out drummers' riffs with their feet while they juggle. The air is white with rigging. A clown, making a flute of his cane, stands on the white hips of a horse as fat as a milkweed pod, while it pitches and yaws around the ring. Perch acts and seal rolls; the rampant chimps; the nodding of the trick ponies; the long, long lions; elephants that almost but never quite step on their trunks. Danny Chapman, the best clown in the show, bounces a ball not inflated enough and passes out flowers, snapping off the heads, leaving only the stems in people's hands.

Prissily he accompanies the band on a drinking straw. And there's Lou Jacobs' built-up conical head, U-shaped red smile, huge tie and little dog (not too big to travel, not too small to think). The cornets play screamers and the trombones do smears. And always the sex, the ecstasy, of the applause.

But the music mourns, too. The clowns pull their wax noses off and stick them on again. The failures in life that they dramatize are no deeper than ours but are better defined. The ballet girls hang by their teeth and their toes; "Atlas" leaps from high up with ropes tied to his heels. The Swiss wire-walker in his most dangerous moments stoops to adjust his pant cuffs—"Oriental" stamina up there, as he bicycles over a cageful of lions. The Boichanovi from Bulgaria construct double towers of themselves four men high from the teeterboard; then one of *five*. And the swaypole is back in the Ringling Brothers repertoire: two poles, with energetic acrobats astride. After scampering up, they slide down headfirst. Eastern Europe has provided the flip acts, the flyers are Latin, the animal trainers German. Though sometimes it seems as if craftsmanship no longer has a place in the world, on the contrary, it may well turn out that practicing a craft will become everybody's aim. If so, the circus is with us to stay. The raciness of show life—long-haired men, buxom women—seems less racy now, but what remains is their loyalty and devotion to these various crafts.

European circuses are more familial in atmosphere than our American brand, and their stars—like the great dapper Russian clown Popov—tend to work from a presumption of good health and good will. Popov depicts a playful, intelligent, well-dressed man at the top of his form, whereas American clowning stresses lunacy, poverty, misery, weirdness. American thrill acts are just that: lean toward the possibility that the man may plunge down before our eyes and die. But in Europe the same performers will use nets or "mechanics" (wires to the roof) because the premium is on dexterity and grace, not simply nerve. Often there is something of a gulf between the European stars brought to this side of the ocean who keep to the friendly, upbeat motif, and the ones who go whole hog instead for our circuses' preference for suffering and the bizarre.

Still, there is a man who combines all virtues and styles: Gunther Gebel-Williams. He chats casually to his umpteen elephants in German, sending them into a dozen maneuvers, and presents horse-riding tigers, elephant-riding tigers, swing-riding tigers, after speeding out to the big cage in the center ring in a white chariot. Lately he has been inserting more violence and dash in his act, but while this may Americanize it somewhat, it's hardly American yet; it's more supernatural. He grins like a changeling as he works—like some primeval, gleeful young water creature thrusting into the world—and as he nears forty, as if growing younger and steelier, he seems to run in the hippodrome more every year.

The show also features Elvin Bale, a brave Floridian who does purist heel catches on the single trapeze and is married to the beautiful Jeanette, who directs hosts of horses in an outré white bustle. Bale does the heel catches

103

for love of his craft; for applause he roars on a motorcycle on a high wire with Victoria Unus dangling and stunting below him. For love of *her* craft Vicki Unus earlier in the show does one-arm planges, pivoting her body over her shoulder a hundred times while hanging from a rope by the same arm. Not long before opening night at Madison Square Garden, Miss Unus's little finger on her right hand had been bitten off by a horse, so it was with pain and apprehension that she performed. Yet just before she went on, when a new midget from Hungary was introduced— Michu, thirty-four years old, thirty-three inches tall—she hunkered down kindly to talk with him. He was standing beside his big duffel bag, which a porter had dumped on the floor, and to those who wouldn't hunker down when they shook hands, he made a deep bow.

It's a loud, shiny show, the smoothest in years. Don Foote's costuming is witty, as always, and right from the start the clowns swivel into the audience and the rings fill up. The trombones march one way and the trumpets another. Put as simply as possible, what these people are trying to do is entertain, astonish and, yes, enlighten us with their trim tumbles, with the tricks, innocence, pathos, forlornness and perfection of their bodies. Their *bodies*— here in the waning decades of the century they are offering us their mere bodies! Bodies of course are an endangered species, but we ourselves, as we know all too well, with our hanging flowerpots and our cats in the window, are endangered also.

WRITING

WILD

Among the booming items
in the book business lately have been volumes on the
problems and the rise of women, on black life and liberation, on radicalism, on Indians, and on what is called
"ecology," often erroneously, by which is meant environmental issues, alarums and wistfulness. With all but the
first of these categories, a publisher's main difficulty has
not only been to find willing readers, but enough writers.
The environment, for example, and in particular the wilderness, was not a splendid and traditional subject like
religion, endowed with the effulgent ponderings of entire
centuries. New as a concern, intellectually marginal, the
product partly of an emergency situation and partly of
nostalgia born from the nation's affluence, it has had no
backlog of dependable interpretation, no cadre of inter-
preters in training. Apart from a few scientists who quickly
had their say, and after the classics of Thoreau and Darwin and various explorers' journals had been reprinted,
who would write the books to satisfy this appetite? So

many writers who in their knockabout careers have evinced an affinity for wild places are primarily novelists. And in fact the wilderness no longer exists at all except in the terms the public allows it to. It's said there are only two places left in the contiguous states that are more than ten miles from some kind of road, and probably it's becoming impossible for any writer to depict from firsthand experience a real wilderness. From now on an act of imagination will be required, equivalent to the effort of a man who is not a war veteran writing a war novel: even if the writer be Stephen Crane, some of the richness of reality is going to be lost. The frontier will be portrayed as merely harsh and not gleeful, or else as simply gleeful and not harsh. With wet feet in the snow, he can perhaps relive a little of the harshness—but how the glee, which comes only from being at home?

Still, the call goes out for somebody to fly to Baffin Island or Baja California for the book clubs or to do a drive-around book here in the States, squeezing into any corner of the continent that may yet appear pristine. Sometimes the proposal is made to me, with a payment being offered many times what I am used to. I'm inclined to accept, believing that driving around is part of a writer's vocation. I know by now that I'm unlikely to find a wilderness, but in looking at the sandhill cranes of Jackson County, Mississippi, the yellow rails of Brazoria County, Texas, I may learn something.

I set off to these wildlife refuges and salt swamps, touring in fat-wheeled marsh buggies and pirogues with motors on them, looking for alligators, chatting with the refuge manager. We stop at a golf club and talk with an old wolf trapper, now the greenskeeper, and pull up by the fence of a Texas prison farm to watch the prisoners being disciplined (it seems to be a local joke). By myself, I do a little walking. The acreage I've come to see may be large or extra-large, but it is not a wilderness, and invariably it is empty; almost no visitors. Where are these book-club readers I'm supposed to be writing my account for? On the highways, certainly, but not out in the bush. The roads are full and the woods empty, or where they aren't, on a few established paths like Vermont's Long Trail, a repair job on the footing costs up to two or three thousand dollars per mile.

How long will these readers continue to miss walking in the woods enough to employ oddballs like me and Edward Abbey and Peter Matthiessen and John McPhee to do it for them? Not long, I suspect. We're a peculiar lot: McPhee long bent to the traces of *The New Yorker*, Matthiessen an explorer in remote regions that would hound most people into a nervous breakdown, Abbey angry, molded by what is nowadays euphemistically called "Appalachia." As a boy, I myself was mute for years, forced either to become acutely intuitive or to take to the woods. By default, we are the ones the phone rings for, old enough to have known real cowboys and real woods. McPhee and I were classmates at prep school. I used to watch him star at basketball; attendance at the games was required, and if we in the bleachers didn't cheer, the headmaster's assistant wrote our names down. But cheered though he was, he too somewhere must have picked up a taste for solitude.

We are old-fashioned craftsmen all, and in our disparate ways children of the thirties, and solitude, among our subjects, should keep us in fish and chips even after the vogue for death-of-nature books has dampened. Perhaps there's rather little to be said about solitude. It amounts to what Saul Bellow once said about loneliness: a plankton upon which the whalelike ego of a novelist must feed. But since such feeding remains a necessity for each of us, reader and writer alike, we seldom lose interest in solitude. At home in Vermont, lounging on my lawn, I look up at a higher tier of land where only black bears live. I'm on the brink of embarking upon still another trip to some bleak national swamp or public forest, and I think, Good God, who needs it? Like anybody else, I'm lonely enough right in the bosom of family and friends. But excitement, the hope of visions and some further understanding— that old, old boondoggle perpetrated by the wilderness— draws me on.

LAMENT
THE
RED WOLF

1

———

Gas rationing is in order, the Environmental Protection Agency suggests. What will young people do? Ordinarily a fuel shortage accompanies a war, when they have various surrogates. It's not really that driving equals living dangerously, however. People drive more dangerously in the Alpes-Maritimes than in America, and in Italy a car itself perhaps can represent more precisely a man's own personality— at least, to hear the honking, it seems so. When I was living in a village in Sicily, the padrone of the lemon groves lying all around would wake up the populace after midnight with the peremptory note of his Ferrari's horn as he sped home. He was signaling to have his front gate opened, and to hasten the job, began a tattoo of toots right as he entered town. But distances, not speed, characterize American driving: trailers, campers and the like. Or a retired couple, as their first project, will set out to tour from coast to coast, reserving a motel room each morning four hundred miles ahead. Youngsters, above all, start off, having the breadth and complexity of the continent to familiarize themselves with.

Geography has glamour in America. The whole excitement of driving here implies some opposite new place to reach, and other nationalities like us for this. The English, arriving in Boston, promptly want to head for Arizona to meet the Navajos. Thomas Wolfe celebrated the cross-country railroad, the auto's smoky, rumbling precursor; and how Walt Whitman would have loved to drive, finally to run plunk up against the shining Pacific. Although there used to seem to be no need to go beyond the sea—whichever sea—because almost everybody's ancestors had crossed over from the other side, those two grand bulky oceans, separated by such a spread of miles, did much to mute for us the sadness of the end of the frontier.

What is ominous is that we know that once they have been instituted, alterations and restrictions in the scope of life are never quite relaxed. Actual rationing may not come to pass, but in the meantime the spontaneity of travel has become a privilege, not a right; a freedom that was traditional has been pinched off. It would be easier to assent to the call for a return to the simple life—long walks, and so on—if we hadn't already made so many localities uninhabitable, on the theory that everybody who lived in them could pop onto the freeway and drive someplace else for a day off. Nixon, jumping into his jet or speeding along the thruways near San Clemente to let off steam, was only a souped-up version of the rest of us.

I have driven clear from east to west and west to east half a dozen times, and yet this closing of the open road strikes me as an immediate personal loss. When my native iconoclasm builds up in me until I want to knock people's hats off, I pile into my car and drive away with the window open, and soon find myself singing "God is good, God is great!" at the top of my lungs into the roaring wind, looking out at the tire recaps along the highway in Pennsylvania—then, two days later, at alligators, which are the spitting image of tire recaps, in the watery Louisiana woods.

This trip I was wolfing, though. I had a hand-cranked siren in the trunk that wolves will answer to, and a wolfish, lunging husky along, whose beastly nostrils at my ear and boisterous snuffles from the back seat kept the car from becoming completely a car. I'd been to Minnesota to see how the black bears manage, because there is some hope for them, and now I wanted to have a look at an officially endangered species, and while I was at it, perhaps at the animal which in America is the worst off, Texas's red wolf. Even with the crush in the world, some creatures do thrive—the scavengers and compleat omnivores like possums and coons, and beasts that move into a disrupted habitat by preference, like cottontails and ground squirrels. Others, more conspicuous—the arrowy, showy predators and hearty herd creatures like buffaloes and prairie dogs—or animals that are too single-minded or delicately attuned, haven't much chance. One's interest swings back and forth between the two groups.

Conservationists assume that a day will come when we will all want to pick up the pieces—that if only they can hold onto such living entities as the green turtle and the right whale for a little while longer, the consensus of civilized opinion will swing behind them. It is a questionable assumption, and so the gloomier, more visceral individuals go instead on the hunch that something may happen whereby finally the saved animals will inherit the earth. This isn't sensible, is misanthropic, and is a view they keep to themselves, but the most vivid observation to be made about animal enthusiasts—both the professionals who work in the field and, in particular, the amateurs—is that they are split between the rosiest, well-adjusted sort of souls and the wounded and lame. (More professionals are rosy, more amateurs are lame.) Animals used to provide a lowlife way to kill and get away with it, as they do still, but, more intriguingly, for some people they are an aperture through which wounds drain. The scapegoat of olden times, driven off for the bystanders' sins, has become a tender thing, a running injury. There, running away—save it, save it—is me: hurt it and you are hurting me.

Wolves are well suited to cupping any wounds that we wish drained. Big and concise enough to command the notice of any dullard, they are aggressive, as the wounded themselves wish to be aggressive. Once passionately persecuted, in just the kind of turnabout which people relish, a wolf can now be taken to represent the very Eden we miss, and being a wolf is thought to be the best at what it does in a world which demands that any creature to receive attention must be the "best." Although in fact red wolves are inferior to other wolves at wolfish deeds, their name "red" adds a cachet, concealing their ineptitude from everybody except their friends.

Luckily for me, the scientist working with these little wolves, Glynn Riley, was not under contract to *The National Geographic*, or otherwise operating under the notion that he should hoard his findings. On the other hand, he wasn't a certified scientist either, but a trapper who simply had interested himself and learned more than the degree-bearing scientists had been able to. This meant, in the first place, that he was suspicious of any writer from the big city because of the campaign of the urban humane societies against the leg-hold steel trap—a threat to his livelihood, as he conceived it, which loomed importantly to him, if not to me. Also he felt none of the curiosity in chatting with me that the full-fledged *National Geographic* biologists are likely to reveal, even as they hold back the yarns and lore they plan to jot down for their own profit at some future date. One can wheedle considerable information from them sideways, so to speak, and it is not as lonely with the *National Geographic* biologists because the rapport goes both ways, whereas after a week or two with a trapper, one begins wishing that maybe he'll ask a question about New York City.

Instead of growing less susceptible to the debilitations of solitude, as I get older I am more so. It's a peculiar life: Tuesday hurrying along Sixth Avenue in New York, Wednesday, after a flight, exploring Dog Canyon in the Big Bend country near the Rio Grande, startling the vultures off a lion-killed deer in a dry streamed overhung

with black persimmon trees. To drive the distances involved helps cushion the switch, but then one runs out
of gumption that much sooner at the site one has come
so far to inspect. More than once I've had to dash away
from scenery that was unimaginably lovely because I
knew my time was up, that if I lingered, my mind, like
Cinderella's, would soon be crawling with transmogrified
mice. I've had crying jags and such, once in the room
which serves as office for water pollution control for the
Louisiana Department of Wildlife and Fisheries, head-
quartered in Baton Rouge. It was an appropriately empty,
watery spot for crying, and funny because to actually deal
with water pollution in Louisiana would require an office
suite the size of the Pentagon. I'd spent a clutch of weeks
with four French-speaking fur trappers in the Cajun salt
marshes that front the Gulf in the southwestern part of
the state, and now after my contact man here in official-
dom got through arguing his budget request for the ensuing
year, we were to set off on a night trip by skiff so that I could
stay awhile with several fresh-water trappers in the
cypress-tupelo gum tree swamps between the Mississippi
River and Lake Maurepas. I couldn't stem the tears.

Air travel and the telephone, too, make for hysteria. A
few spins of the dial and we can talk to almost anybody
in the world, and in towns like Hackberry or Buras,
Louisiana, or Alpine, Texas, at the first strong pinch of
loneliness I've known that I could jump into my Hertz
Ford and hop a plane for home. The trouble is, at home
I've often wanted to catch a plane for Alpine—to be back

in Dog Canyon again listening to the javelinas yap and fuss; then, uneasy there, might want to streak for Philadelphia. A friend of mine does let this panic take possession of him. His acquaintances in Hawaii, Los Angeles and London hear from him, the times being rough and events going badly. Since he is an endearing chap, they say yes, he can come, and await his next move. He's reassured by all the invitations and calls or writes his other friends to tell them he is going to Hawaii, London, Los Angeles or Mexico City. He calls the airport for fare and timetable information, but in the end, more frequently than not, relaxed at last by the show of affection, he goes nowhere at all.

In Minnesota, Lynn Rogers, the bear expert, had been rather guarded with me, as though he were feeling vulnerable himself and did not welcome the possibility that somebody else might get a handle on him which properly ought to be his. By contrast, Glynn Riley had no suspicions of me as a lay psychologist, didn't care what I thought of him and wasn't concerned with the riddles of motivation. Instead, he was alert to the good name of his profession, and while he told me freely about his boyhood, his screw-ups in school, and courting Pat, his wound-up, stringbean wife—she has a certain flash and dazzle to her eyes and hair, and used to fold herself into the trunk of his car to get into the drive-in movies when they were kids—with the equanimity of a man at peace with himself, he would do this only on his own front porch. Never would he let me bounce about the country with him on his regular rounds, as Rogers had, checking traps and palavering with the ranchers, lest I see a trapped creature and write of its struggles. I couldn't convince him that an exposé of trapping was very low on my list of priorities; I'd seen plenty of trapping and knew that if the fellow wasn't one of a kind, like Riley, he was probably by now a grandfather who wouldn't be around by the time the controversy resolved itself. Similarly, the trapper employed by the wolf scientists in Minnesota, an old-timer who catches the wolves that they can't, won't let anybody else watch how he works. If he is in his pickup with one of the Ph.D. candidates, he will drive past a likely trap-site, giving no sign that he has noticed it, and stop a hundred yards beyond, leaving the young man in the truck and walking back to set the device with his back turned, lest at this late date these doctoral scholars, discovering his secrets, might desert their latter-day vocation for the sake of becoming a master trapper and compete with him.

In spite of being thin-skinned, Rogers had liked lecturing on bears and appearing on television and in the papers, but Glynn Riley had let me drive down to see him solely in the hope that I might pry loose from the Bureau of Sport Fisheries and Wildlife in Washington his appropriated funding, and more too, so that he could put radios on the wolves and hire a spotting plane and someone to help him. As I had seen, they were being as slow as a taffy-pull up there, but he was also sick of blathering to newspapermen—sick of their errors, ignorance, perfunctoriness, misemphasis—and though I explained that letters might accomplish what he wanted,* that I had hopes of doing more with the wolves than merely publicize them, he remained correct with me, not to be cozened.

The dog-wolf family is thought to have originated in North America, migrated to Eurasia, where the gray wolf defined itself as a prodigy of the Northern Hemisphere, and then returned. Some biologists think that red wolves may be descended from a primitive wolf that stayed in North America during this diaspora and were hounded into the southeast lip of the continent by the returning grays. Others speculate that they are an offshoot of a worldwide race of primitive wolves of the early Pleistocene which have disappeared elsewhere; or, on the contrary, that they are a product of the devious ice-age geography blocked out by the glaciers which did so much differentiating among animal species. Another theory is that the red wolf sprouted from a common ancestor with the coyote in the Pliocene, and is not directly from the gray wolf's line. Coyotes, like Old World jackals, are "brush wolves" that became miniaturized for pursuing smaller prey in broken country where a hefty predator might not operate as well. They can put up with hotter temperatures—ranging into Central America—but not with the deep snows and freezes that arctic gray wolves know.

Red wolves are short-coated and long-eared, with stilty, spindly legs for coursing through the southern marshes

---

* Sure enough, writing to Washington, I did elicit the funding he had wanted, but along with the funding came a supervisory bureaucracy, which pleased him less.

or under tall forests. They have the neck ruff, almond eyes and wide nose pad of other wolves, but not the massive head and chest, and so their angular ears and legs seem to stick out plaintively. Anatomically their brains are primitive, almost foxlike among the canids, and they have impressed naturalists as being as rather rudimentary animals, fragile in their social linkups, not very clever, unenterprising and almost easy to trap. Besides the pacing gait that they share with larger wolves and a flat dash, they bound along like modest rocking horses, standing up on their hind legs to peer over a patch of tall weeds. They are an unemphatic, intermediate sort of animal, behaviorally like wolves, ecologically more like coyotes. They howl like wolves, not like coyotes, and snarl when threatened instead of silently gaping the mouth, as coyotes do. They scout in little packs, unlike coyotes, which have stripped away a good deal of the pack instinct for better secrecy in crowded country and better efficiency at gleaning small game. A grown male weighs about sixty pounds, midway between a coyote's thirty or forty and a gray wolf's average of eighty pounds; but skinny as he is, the red wolf can live on a coyote's diet of cotton rats and marsh rabbits, and whereas a gray wolf needs about ten temperate square miles to feed himself—coyotes can get along as densely distributed as one every square mile— the red wolf again is in between. Five square miles supplies his food, and ten to forty is enough to stretch his legs and psyche with other members of the pack, about half what a pack of Minnesota timber wolves requires.

The earliest observers—William Bartram in 1791, and

118

Audubon and Bachman in 1851—were definite on the subject of a smallish, darkish, long-legged wolf inhabiting the region from Florida to what is now central Texas, and north to the Ohio River. It was primarily a forest beast, piney in its affinities. The first government biologists of this century, men like Vernon Bailey and Edward Goldman, backed up the idea of a specifically southern wolf still more strongly, although the animals on the eastern seaboard had been exterminated already, and were gone everywhere east of the Mississippi by the 1920s. They did range the Ozarks and the river bottoms of Louisiana and the East Texas prairies, but because some of these latter had started hybridizing with an invading legion of coyotes, a body of opinion claimed that red wolves might never have existed at all except as hybrids of a coyote-gray wolf cross, or maybe as local grays, colored to suit the climate, in much the way that "white" wolves developed in the north. Since gray wolves possess such a fastidious sense of self that a cross of the sort would be a rarity, the rival proposition was offered that though red wolves might have existed as a true species at some point, they'd crossed themselves into extinction even before white men arrived.

Wolves are special beasts, so variable genetically that they partly live on disguised as dogs. Dogs, too, dance attendance on a breadwinner, cheerfully accepting the ups and downs of life with a master just as wolves stick with the pack, and bark and rush at an intruder close to the "den," otherwise marking their passage through life semantically with squirts of pee. If dogs were to inherit the

earth they would quickly turn into wolves again; and coyotes carry the flag for wolves most directly, becoming
bushy-necked and wolfish in appropriately remote surroundings, or little more than wild dogs when they live close
to a city. Indeed, gray wolves would need only a nod from
the voters to get a foothold in corners of their old range—
Maine, for instance. Brought in, they would soon be at
home, parceling up the timberland wherever the human
populace is thin, until the deer found themselves in a
density of two or three hundred per wolf.

But red wolves are so far gone by now—none has been
photographed in the wild since 1934, and they are considered present in pure form in only two of Texas's two
hundred and fifty-four counties—that the main effort to
protect them involves not only shielding them from human intervention but from encroachment and dilution by
coyotes. This situation is unusual. The rarest breeds of
ferret, parrot, and so on, even manatees and prairie chickens, depleted in numbers though they are, seldom require
protection from other animals, and it is this peculiar
rattle-headedness—that these last wolves will so amenably
let a coyote mount them—which has called into question
their right to be regarded as a species. Mostly the museum
scientists, such as Barbara Lawrence of Harvard, rather
than the outdoor workers, have been occupied with chal-
lenging them, but recently a formidable young taxonomist
at the University of Kansas, Ronald Nowak, with a friend
named John Paradiso from the National Museum in Washington, has computerized a much larger body of evidence
than Lawrence's and has taken up the cudgels for them.

The current majority view is to return to the belief that
Canis rufus (called *Canis niger* for a while, but scientific
names sometimes change more frivolously than common
ones) is indeed a discrete creature, only lately decimated.

Nearer the East Coast, there were no other predators
to replace the wolves when they had been killed off, but
west of the Mississippi, coyotes from the plains slid in as
soon as the shattered packs stopped defending an area.
Coyotes could withstand the poisoning and trapping campaigns better, and the hard logging that the settlers did
among the old-growth trees actually benefited them by
breaking down the forest canopy. According to the evidence of skulls in the National Museum, the red wolves
of Missouri, northern Arkansas and eastern Oklahoma
met their end in good order as a species, not mating with
the coyotes as they were superseded. (It is a textbook
theory that a true species is supposed to preserve its racial
purity even more stubbornly in a border area under pressure.) But around the turn of the century, on the Edwards
Plateau of central Texas where the same blitzkrieg of
white settlers from the East was followed by an invasion
of coyotes from every other direction, the demoralized
red wolves for some reason began to accept coyotes as
their sexual partners, and in the delirium of catastrophe
created with them a "Hybrid Swarm." This "Swarm"
thereupon moved eastward slowly, as ordinary coyotes
were doing anyway at every latitude clear into Canada—
and naturally was irresistible. Bigger, "redder" than coyotes, with such a piquancy of wolf blood already, these
hybrids absorbed the wolves of Texas's Hill Country and

Big Thicket all the more readily. They bred with true wolves and true coyotes and wild-running domestic dogs (even a few escaped pet dingos)—anything they met and couldn't kill—becoming ever more adaptable, a shoal of skilled survivors in a kind of canine Injun-territory situation.

The beaver trappers in the West had hiked out of the mountains and switched to hunting buffalo when the beaver were gone. The buffalo hunters were soon wolfers as well, and bounty-hunted them for a living after they had run through the buffalo. They sold the skins and paved the mudholes in their roads with heaped wolf bones, so many thousands were killed. Throughout the 1800s strychnine was the poison used. Then a drastic potion, sodium fluoroacetate, known as "1080," was introduced, and by the 1940s, a device called the "getter gun," which when implanted in the ground fires cyanide gas into the animal's open mouth when it pulls on a trigger knob baited with scent. From 1915 on, most of the wolfers were employed by the U.S. Biological Survey, which under the umbrella of the Interior Department eventually metamorphosed into the Bureau of Sport Fisheries and Wildlife. Thus by a piece of bureaucratic irony the same corps responsible for reducing the Midwestern red wolf to its final extremity is now the agency in charge of trying to preserve it. Even some of the personnel have been the same, which gives credence to the frequent complaints of calculated foot-dragging that conservationists have made.

To a taxonomist who looks at skulls of the period the record now seems plain as to how succinctly coyotes sup-

planted wolves in the hardwoods bottomlands along the
Mississippi and in the Ozark Mountains. But the salaried
wolfers naturally preferred to continue to see themselves,
like the old-timers, as dealing with wolves, and so they
kept on totting up an annual kill of thousands of "red
wolves" in the official tabulation. As late as 1963, 2,771
were reported to have been done away with in the federal
program of control. The year before, however, an obscure
dissenter, Dr. Howard McCarley of Austin College, Texas,
had published his contention that many of these were
either coyotes or hybrids, and that the red wolf was nearly
gone. Once his discovery was confirmed, the received
opinion among biologists, who had taken so cavalier a
view of *Canis rufus* until then, reversed abruptly to the
notion that the creature may well have existed, but no
longer. Since there was nothing to be done about it, the
poisoning was allowed to continue even in the Texas
coastal counties where in fact a few survived, till 1966.
Fortunately two Ontario scientists, taking the matter more
seriously than most of the Americans, journeyed about
one summer in the meantime playing recorded wolf howls
in wild places and listening to the answers that they got—
sundry barking mutts, coyotes and coydogs. They were
privately financed and soon ran out of funds, but they did
learn that while McCarley had been right about the broad
belt of territory he had studied, down on the muggy coast
between the Vermilion River in western Louisiana and
the Brazos in Texas a tiny remnant of voices were answering their Canadian wolves in kind. What with the lengthy
delay in publishing these findings in a recondite journal

123

(like McCarley's, earlier), and of bringing them to the attention of the federal specialists, not until 1968 was an organized recovery effort initiated, and not until 1973 was enough money provided to really begin. The scientific method depends upon a scoffing skepticism on the part of rival investigators to puncture a weak argument, but one reason why the biologists did not do more for the red wolf is that so many of them dillydallied while they scoffed.

Part of the appeal of Southeast Texas is that some of its residents tend to deprecate the charms of the place. They'll say that the landscape is mosquito-bitten and unlovely, the colors washed out, that a tourist who wants scenery ought to move on. For a hundred years an army of Texans have believed themselves to be a Chosen People on the grounds of their good fortune—rather like the Victorian British, and in contradistinction to the Jews, for example, who historically have interpreted *mis*fortune to be the insignia of blessedness. Many people have believed that they were Chosen, but none more baldly than the Texans. Standing one evening in the Chisos Basin, an old Apache stronghold which is probably the pearl of the western section of the state, I must have looked affected by the colors because I heard a Dallas fellow drawl behind me, "Well, you think you'll buy it?"

Minnesota had seemed fairly familiar—bleaker and flatter than northern New England, wilder than around my home in Vermont, but not more so than northern Maine, which has a moose herd three times the size of

Minnesota's and a wilderness region three times as large. Lakes were interspersed through a balsam fir and white pine forest, and the natives had that clamped-down modesty cold weather brings, because you can't cultivate too grandiose an opinion of yourself when a three-foot snowfall at any time for half the year may shut you in. In Isabella, Minnesota, there was an individual called The Pig Farmer because of his supposed smell, who when the spring floods came would slosh around in two feet of water in his swamp cabin, eat cold food, and sleep in a wet bed instead of bothering to move to higher ground. Maybe nobody else can be as glum as a Great Lakes Finlander, but near my house in Vermont is a barn with a whole cavern smashed in it which the farmer himself fashioned one night by driving his bulldozer against the wall when he heard that his youngest son, too, was going to leave the farm.

People who are bundled up much of the time, with stacks of firewood half the size of the house, and the sense that things will most likely go wrong if they haven't already: this is the America which stretches next to the Canadian boundary from the Atlantic Ocean to the Great Plains. The warm-weather rain forest of the Pacific might alter even a woodsman's outlook substantially, and, otherwise, the Rockies will give him big ideas, but what happens where the plains begin is that all of a sudden there are no trees. *No trees!* People started wearing big hats not simply because the brims were shady and wouldn't catch in the branches, but to help break up the landscape. It was a vast change, and in a huge country without

125

forests to enforce a different perspective, many of them got to feeling big in the britches as well as in the head. Indeed, the big got bigger. Whereas in the woods that fellow with the swamp shanty and two cabbagey acres owns everything the eye can see, on the prairie it takes a rich man to feel so proprietary.

Down in Texas, the hats, the vistas and the britches, the distances to be ridden, were more expansive still. To be thirsty in Texas was a powerful thirst. The rich grew filthy rich, but before that the Indians, whom the Texans dispatched with an implacable efficiency that was the envy of Indian-haters everywhere, had included some of the continent's stiffest tribes. Not only Apaches, but Comanches, and not only Comanches, but the Attacapas and Karankawas of the Gulf Coast, who in the early years were rumored to enjoy a man-bake as much as a clambake, eating a castaway's buttocks and arms right in front of him as he died.

The "Kronks," as the white men were wont to call the Karankawas (or, in an earlier, more authentic spelling, "Carancahueses"), were a robust people described as standing almost seven feet tall, with slender hands and feet, sensitive faces, and hair to their shoulders, with snake rattles tied in it and bangs in front, who swam superbly and cruised between the islands and sandbars of Galveston Bay in little fleets of dugout pirogues. They communicated with smoke signals—Y's and V's, diverging, curling, spiraling columns or twin zigzags—and employed a six-foot cedar bow with a three-foot goose-feathered arrow. Two families might travel together in a pirogue with a small deck at either end and the baggage heaped in the middle, erecting at night a single shelter of skins thrown over poles on the beach. They worshiped the sun, and on ceremonial occasions blew the smoke of a fire in seven sacred directions. They had a personalized god named "Pichini" and a dread god "Mel," in whose grim celebrations they played a dismal-sounding stringed instrument five feet long, which bellowed like an alligator. For gayer festivities they had a tambourine made from a tortoise shell and a reed whistle. They talked in whistles and sign language as well as words, and counted on their fingers, going from the pinkie to the thumb, which was the "father." They were a voluptuous people, the women grabbing for the penis of an enemy's corpse. It was said that they masturbated a good deal, and their name Karankawa was generally translated as "dog-lovers," because of the horde of voiceless dogs they kept, though their detractors claimed that the love went to even further extremes. The Lipan Apaches called them "those-who-walk-in-water" because they shot fish while wading, rather than from a boat. The Tonkawas called them "the wrestlers" because they liked to wrestle and were good at it. They wore a breechclout of Spanish moss, with a wreath of palm leaves as a hat and perhaps a cock partridge's feather behind one ear. They slept wrapped in deerskins and kept their firesticks in a skin bundle, used wooden spoons and fishbone needles, and red and black pots with conical bottoms that would stand upright in the sand. They ate seafood and every kind of meat, from buffaloes to skunks and reptiles—nursing their children for years to shelter

127

them from this rough diet. The children, their foreheads sometimes flattened as a form of decoration, played with wooden dolls, and the adults tattooed blue circles on their own cheeks, and lines from eye to ear or parallel lines descending from the mouth. With vermilion they accentuated their eyes and striped themselves red and black and white, unmarried girls with the simplest, thinnest line, but married individuals decorating themselves with flowers, birds and animals, and hanging colored stones and conch shells from their ears and the wings of the nose.

The Karankawas smelled of alligator grease, which was their chief protection from the bugs. After the whites had outgunned them, they hid in the thorn-brush thickets and behind the endless screen of man-high roseau cane. Since they had fought against the Comanches and Jean Lafitte's pirates, as well as against more orthodox settlers, and since they had numbered probably only about four hundred warriors when La Salle first landed on the Texas shore to establish a fort in 1685, they were all gone before the Civil War, when settlement really started. The last canoeful of able-bodied men deliberately paddled for the open sea during a storm, the legend goes, and the few women and children left begged their way on foot along the coast to Mexico.

Wolves, too, were a force that molded early Texas, and the optimists would claim that if we can just hold onto a smattering of them, when the time comes that people want to pick up the pieces we will have them around as a force to observe once again. The difficulty is that though there are as many buffaloes alive as the buffalo reserves can hold, buffaloes are not a force any more; indeed, buffaloes not in the millions may not *be* buffaloes. Neither are Big Brown Bears a force, nor Mounted Indians. That former midcontinental prairie community of mounted Indians, gaudily iconic big brown bears, and buffaloes and rattlesnakes and eagles and gray wolves that once existed centering around what is now Nebraska and Wyoming represents our idea of the pre-white New World better than the coastal or woodland aboriginal cultures do, and we all turn a bit sorrowful, reading of the buffaloes shot by the millions for their tongues, of whole dramatic nations of plains Indians starved or served up smallpox or ridden under the ground. Yet we wouldn't then and wouldn't now have had it any other way. What could we have possibly done with all those goofy buffaloes besides shoot them right off? Land of opportunity, land for the huddled masses—where would the opportunity have been without the genocide of those Old-Guard, bristling Indian tribes?

A pause is necessary when speaking in defense of wolves for some mention of their fearful destructiveness. The settlers had good reason to be afraid of wolves, the same reason that the Indians had for howling to each other when they surrounded an isolated cabin: wolves digging under a dead man's cairn to wolf down his spoiling remains, wolves disemboweling the family cow, feeding on her thighs and abdominal fat, burying their heads inside her, although her entrails lay unbroken and she was still alive and watching them. When wild game was no longer available, wolves killed the new livestock prodigiously—such stupid, lavish, feasty beasts presented to them on a tray. They soon cast off their wilderness inhibition against killing too much to eat; there was no sating them, and for a cattleman no living with them—at least the big buffalo lobos. It was either them or him. No honest-minded naturalist can peer at a caged wolf without recognizing in the old sense its wicked air. That sharp and fabled nose hooding the teeth, the bright eyes all the more dangerous for being downcast, the uncannily tall legs and twitching ears—these, with its lugubrious howl, were what the pioneers feared.

The first settler straggled into the wilderness with a single-shot rifle, leading a couple of mules, with a crate of brood hens on the back of one and two piglets in a sack to balance the load, some seed corn, potatoes and soldier beans, and dragging a long-suffering cow with a half-grown bull at her heels which the fellow hoped might manage to freshen her again before he butchered it. In the north, he settled in a beaver meadow where a little wild hay grew, and planted his potato peelings, living off boiled cowslips, sour dock, dandelion greens, Indian turnips and goldthread roots in the meantime. In red-wolf country, he lived in a hot hut with a scrap of cloth hanging across the door hole to fend the mosquitoes off, and saw his cattle, too, turn gray with malaria or bog down dead. He was afraid of wolves. The prairie was theirs, not his, and if they swept through in cavalry style, mocking his gun, and killed his mules, he was in a bad way. If they killed his cow, his children would have no milk; if they drove the deer out of the neighborhood and killed his chickens and hogs, the whole family might starve. A bachelor mountain man, wrapped in hides, here today and gone tomorrow with a pack of curs, could afford to be more nonchalant; he had no kids wandering alone along the streambank poking at the muskrats with a stick, and if he stretched his lungs at night he could holler from his bedroll louder than the hooting packs. When he shot a deer he tied his neckerchief to it to keep the wolves away until he lugged the last of it to camp. Still, sometimes these self-sustaining hobos were the ones who reported the attacks; the wolves were hunting something else and in their speed and happiness (they have been seen to jump up on the rump of a running moose and briefly ride there) happened to blunder on the man and turn toward him. In Kipling's *Jungle Book*, wolves were "the Free People."

A real wolfer lived for his wolves, trailed them for days, smelling their pee and fingering their toeprints to distinguish the bitch from her mate, slept out in order to waylay them on the trail, and when he'd shot them both, walked from his hiding place to scalp them and strip off their skins in an act quick as sex, leaving the white frames grinning in the grass. That yodeling, streaking wolf—he strung up snares that yanked it into the air and kept it hanging there, upright as an effigy, choking, kicking, till he came in the morning and hugged and punched it and cut its throat, or bound its jaws with barbed wire and carried it home across his horse to tie to a tree in the dooryard to tease for a week.

Here in littoral Texas the pioneers found an old-growth forest of large sweet gums, elms, loblolly and longleaf pines, hackberry trees and beech and oak. Wild violets and blackberries grew where the trees gave out, and then the prairie extended toward the sea: bluestem bunch grasses, Indian grass, gama grass and switch grass, with bluebells and milkweed spreading blue and white during the spring and buttercups and Indian pinks under these, the terrain broken by occasional sand knolls covered with yaupon and myrtle brush where the wolves denned and hid out. Next came a marsh of spunkweed, cattails, cut-grass and the same spartina that the colonists on the Atlantic shore had fed to their livestock. A bayshore ridge fronted the Gulf, beyond which the wolves and pioneers and Indians crabbed and beachcombed, collecting stunned redfish by the wagonload after a storm. Wagonloads of oysters, too; and in the bayous mullet seethed among gar, catfish and bullheads. Out in the tides were weakfish, black drum, channel bass, gafftopsail cats, sand trout. Summer was the fishing season; in the winter everybody lived on wildfowl and game. Prairie chickens could be caught by hand when they got drunk on fermented china-berries; so could the geese when their wings froze to-gether when the rain blew cold.

There was yellow fever, and hurricanes that washed away entire hamlets, and influenza in the winds and hock-deep water that the cattle still stand in. The wolves fed on sick waterfowl from everywhere north to above Hud-son's Bay. They still eat sick birds, mainly cripples from the hunting months, which is when the ranchers make their tax money, charging ten dollars a day per hunter. Red-winged blackbirds and robins continue to flock in million-bird masses, and blue and snow geese arrive from Canada by the tens of thousands, along with teal, gadwalls, canvasbacks, pintails, shovelers and widgeons. The federal government has a bird refuge at Anahuac in Chambers County and two near Angleton in Brazoria County and one in Cameron Parish, Louisiana. The managers of these burn over the brush to plant millet and other goose food, and bring in cattle to keep the grass cropped green and short and to chop puddles in the ground with their hard hooves.

It seemed unbelievable that these last uncompromised wolves should have been discovered here in the salt marshes—next to Houston, Galveston and Beaumont, Texas's most industrial and populated section—instead of in the piney woods and hillbilly thickets always listed as their home. Metro Houston grew by six hundred thousand during the 1960s to a total of two million people, America's third largest port by tonnage; yet the wolves had ranged within Harris County itself and beside Galveston Bay and over in Jefferson County, within sight of some of the new subdivisions, through intensively productive rice fields, next to several of the state's earliest oil strikes, such as Spindletop.

Oil wells pump like nodding grasshoppers, bird watchers creep about on the lookout for avocets and phalaropes, and now that the deer are mostly gone, the wolves chew on stillborn calves and the carcasses of bloated steers that died of anaplasmosis. It was the last place the authorities

133

had thought to look (for the debunkers, still a debating point), but the industrial buzz, the waterways and highways may have served to delay the coyotes for a little while. The older wolfers I dropped in on mentioned animals weighing ninety pounds or more which they hunted half a century ago with their July and Goodman hounds— roping them or clubbing them in the water when they took to a bayou to escape the dogs. Nowadays the wolves altogether add up to only one or two hundred sorry smaller specimens, because these final marshes are so mosquito-ridden that a calf, for example, may smother from the balls of insects that fasten inside its nose. Heartworms kill or invalid the grown-up wolves, plugging up the heart valves so that they suffer seizures if they run, and hookworms starve the pups. Tapeworms, spiny-headed worms and sarcoptic mange plague them indiscriminately, the spring floods drown their dens, the summer heat renders them somnambulistic and the saw grass rips their fur until their tails are naked as a rat's. In Chambers County alone there are ten cattle ranches of better than ten thousand acres, but the only cattle that can survive the bugs and watery winter footing are an indigenous mongrel Brahma breed.

Still, the ranchers have built many windmill-driven wells that bring fresh water to the wolves and other wildlife as well as to the cattle. The U.S. Soil Conservation Service has constructed raised cow walks above the standing water, and the oil companies have laid oystershell-based roads running upon embankments which provide the wolves with direct access nearly everywhere. Where the sand knolls that used to be their safe haven have been bulldozed away, windbreaks of salt cedar, huisache and Cherokee rose have been planted that fulfill the same purpose. Better still are the innumerable miles of canal banks channeling water to the rice fields, in which a pair of wolves will excavate their various emergency holes to foil a flood or hunter, a practice which also cuts down on puppy parasites.

Rice farming has introduced a "horn of plenty," as Glynn Riley calls it, in the way of rodents. The fields stand fallow every third year, and when they are plowed and reflooded the rice and barn and cotton rats and gobbly mice and big and baby rabbits must scrabble out across the levees to another field in a frenzied exodus which the wolves attend delightedly—just as up north in dairy country, coyotes will follow a farmer's mower at haying time to bolt the running mice, or follow his manure spreader to eat the afterbirths which are included in the mess. But the wolves' best staple lately is another creature tendered up to them by man, the nutria. Nutria are furry water rodents five times the size of a muskrat, and locally more catholic in habitat and diet. Introduced from Argentina to Avery Island, Louisiana, in the 1930s by a Tabasco Sauce mogul who dabbled in natural history, they escaped during a hurricane, and being tolerant of brackish water, made their way successfully along the edge of the Gulf and the Intracoastal Canal, reaching the Rio Grande around 1967. They are a resource in Louisiana—the pelts are worth four or five dollars apiece—but in Texas they are shot as pests because they burrow through the levees and breed exuberantly and eat a lot of rice. They leave fingery tracks—have delicate fingers which can pluck up a single grain of rice—though, when abroad, they are so clumsy that they have been a blessing to the beleaguered alligators as well as the red wolves. The gators grab them in the water and the wolves snatch them in the fields at night when they venture out to feed, and for the wolves there is a nice balance to it because whenever the water gets so high that the nutria achieve a degree of maneuverability, the dry-ground rats are in a panic.

In spite of this abundant provender, coyotes have now seized all but two of the last seven counties under study; there is talk of a "Dunkirk Operation" to salvage a few wolves and whisk them to some sanctuary island such as Matagorda (already teeming with coyotes)—or, as it soon seemed to me, there may be no hope. It may not matter much if we bear in mind the continentwide accomplishments of coyotes in resetting wild areas; these wolves have been grist for the mill, making them bigger and "redder." But such considerations did not temper my irritation at the officials I met who should have cared about what was happening and didn't. The arrangements of the national Wild Animal Propagation Trust to distribute red wolves for a breeding program among cooperating zoo directors had collapsed without getting started. A noted biochemist in Minneapolis who had been interested in doing blood protein studies of the species had been forced to quit for lack of funding. The State of Texas had made no move to resurrect the wolves from unprotected varmint status, or even to make legally permissible the little gestures of help that Riley was receiving from a couple of local enthusiasts. It was both sad and comic; he was entirely on his own—other federal agencies in the neighborhood, and even other chains of command within the Fish and Wildlife Service, seemed indifferent to the matter—yet, as a trapper, he had faith that here in Chambers and Jefferson counties his lone trapline could halt the tide.

Riley lives in the small town of Liberty, and grew up in Wortham in the East Texas brush not far away. His father did some trading in scrub horses and thin cows, and if there wasn't any money in the house it still was a good life for a boy. Now he's thirty-eight, calls his father Pappy and has that cowpoke look of not putting much weight on the ground when he walks. His face is trim and small, his body slim, his hair curly and neat and his voice mild. Like many wildlife men, he prefers being inconspicuous, and nature has given him the wherewithal. After a good supper he'll say that he's "full as a tick." He hasn't finished college yet, having dropped out several times, and is country-religious, so that although he is subject to more than his share of professional frustrations, if he is speaking bitterly and doing a slow burn, suddenly in midsentence he'll undergo a change and say of the other individual in an altered tone, "But bless his heart." "The good Lord gave the wolf forty-two teeth to eat with," he says in the same folksy way; and broadcasts wolf howls from his tape recorder on the telephone to callers. "Sounds like a pack of Indians." He says a mountain with a wolf on it stands a little taller, and that a wolf represents everything a man wants to be. "He's free, he's a traveler, he's always on the move, he kills his food. He's *worth* three hundred deer."

With none of the pained air of a late bloomer, Riley instead seems simply different in this age of Ph.D.'s, and himself suggests that someday his own head ought to be nailed on the wall at the Smithsonian Institution alongside the red wolf's. He is a first-rate trapper, has killed "a jillion" coyotes for the government, and therefore is as skilled at politicking with the old ranchers and trappers as any government agent is going to be. Since he is not a cosmopolitan man, his worst difficulty has probably been in dealing with what ought to be his natural constituency, the conservationists "up East," that redoubtable big-city crew of letter writers whom other scientists have rallied to the cause of the whooping crane, brown pelican, and what not.

From the start trapping has been his passion—on the first day of his honeymoon he insisted upon running his trapline—and he used to measure the tracks of the coyotes in Wortham against the sizable wolf tracks in Stanley Young and Edward Goldman's standard book, *The Wolves of North America*, discovering right as a teenager that these were no longer any variety of wolf, though everybody around still bragged them up as such. He knew of one old beech tree down next to the Trinity River which still carried the claw marks of a black bear that decades ago had climbed it, and knew an old hunter who as a boy had crawled into the briar jungle there after two hounds, thinking they had treed a squirrel, when, lo and behold, one dog jumped over his head to

get away and he saw the bear sitting with its back against
the tree, swatting the remaining pooch. Of course no bears
are left in Texas now within six hundred miles for Riley
to see, and his bitterest experience as a boy was when he
had to sell his rifle and borrow a friend's one fall, in order
to pay the landowner's fee, when he wanted to go hunting.

He loved the howling, the matching of wits, and went
to work for the Bureau, eventually being put in charge of
these last wolves because he'd grown so good at nabbing
coyotes. He's in the position of knowing more about them
than anybody else, yet watching a succession of schooled
young men arrive to make their academic names studying
the animal before it vanishes. They must turn to him for
help, as do the cameramen and journalists who show up
in Liberty, and he's evolved a quietly noncompetitive attitude, putting the fun of his work ahead of the rivalries of
a career. He traps a few wolves to attach radio collars to,
and traps calf-killing wolves when the ranchers complain,
before they get caught in one of the mangling four-trap
clusters that the ranchers set. (The old method was to
drag a dead cow roundabout, strewing chunks of tallow
laced with strychnine behind it.) Mostly, though, he traps
coyotes, especially prophylactically along the edge of the
Big Thicket where the middling tracks of the hybrid
swarm already have met and mingled with the wolves'
large pads.

WOLF AT WORK, says a sign in Riley's office. He claims
he "probably would have amounted to something" if he
hadn't become fascinated with wolves, but that the country "wouldn't be complete" without them. With people

already wall-to-wall, he frankly couldn't comprehend why anyone who was enough like him to show up at his door in the first place would want to live in New York City for much of the year. He was uncomfortably amazed, and every morning talked to me at first as if he were seated in a dentist's chair—I being the dentist—so that his role in whatever I had in mind achieving for him professionally could be over and done with. My lunging husky did serve as a recommendation. Riley laughed at how very furry he was, although in Minnesota, where the dog had also served to break the ice with the predator men (everywhere he tended to offend the ranchers and the farmers), they would immediately begin to talk about a wolf pup they knew back in the bush that was about his size and shade of gray.

Another favorable factor for me was that I'd read some of the literature of this infant science of predator ethology. A poorly, skimpy showing it makes, on the whole —perhaps a good month's read—but few of the journalists who seek out these field men have bothered to look into it at all, and since the field men themselves are not readers outside the particular pocket of their specialty, they are impressed when somebody has taken the trouble. Besides, as boyish as I was (like Riley, I had the sense that these adventurous predators, just as they *eat* all other animals, somehow *contain* all other animals)—still trying morning and night to catch sight of a wolf, peering into the spoil-bank thickets in the rice fields just as I had done thirty years before, speeding across the greasewood West as a youngster en route to Los Angeles on the Super Chief:

by midmorning he would have managed to relax with me.

As kids both of us had climbed to many "caves," which usually proved just to be stains on the face of the rock when we reached them, but hoping to find some magic beast, a cougar or a wolverine, whatever the continent's legends might contain. So now in the evening he took me out to a coyote family's rendezvous, where with the siren we got them howling. Out wolfing again at dawn, we tried to provoke the soundless wolves, but instead it was the snow geese from white-wolf country, wheeling in platters by the thousands, that answered us. We saw coots in the ditches and an alligator so long it looked like two, half in, half out of the water, and more serrate and flat-looking than I'd anticipated. We saw fish popping in Oyster Bayou, and crabs and fat brown water snakes, and an armadillo with a tiny pointed head and papery ears; saw pelicans flying, and wavy lines of white ibises and cormorants, and roseate spoonbills like scoops of strawberry ice cream high in the air, and plenty of mink and otter tracks. Otters lope in a way that even in the form of prints communicates their speedy eagerness.

Riley himself walked rapidly, hunkering down to feel the depressions left by a wolf's toes. He bent right to the ground to smell its scenting station—a wolf's squirt smells milder, not as musky as a coyote's—to distinguish how much time had passed. The far-flung spatters were a diagram for him. He loves toes, hopping with his hands, his fingers in the toes, and never now encounters a wolf or coyote that he can't catch if he wishes to. Often he chooses not to, unless he wants to shift them around, but

141

in any part of Texas he can envision the land much in the way that coyotes do, knowing where to find their prints and how to catch those toes. He's like a managerial cowboy, with wolves and coyotes for his cows.

His traps have toothless offset jaws, with a long swiveled drag to minimize the damage done. He attaches a bit of cloth steeped in tranquilizer for the wolf to mouth so that it will sleep. Sometimes, too, he removes a spring to weaken the bite, and adjusts the pan until the jaws close at a touch, so not the slender leg but the resilient paw is pinched. He boils the traps in a black dye, then coats them with beeswax, and has a shed full of dark-glass bottles of wolf, coyote and bobcat urine, with bits of anal gland chopped in, or powdered beaver castor and beaver oil—two universal lures from his old haunts along the Trinity—to sprinkle on a mudbank above the trap, although in fact the wolves are gullible enough to step into a trap lying open on the ground if it is placed well, and coyotes, though cleverer, are nearly as curious as they are clever, so that anything that stinks may draw some of them in.

Wolves scratch at a scent post after wetting it, whereas bobcats scratch beforehand, and neither is especially intrigued by the other's sign, but to trap either animal he employs the scent of an interloper of the same species. Wolves love to cross into the territory of another pack and leave their mark to razz the residents, like kids painting their colors on a rival school. Some of the feral dogs he traps run snapping at him, but wolves and coyotes are dumbstruck as he approaches, and after a bark or two will do anything to avoid offending him. Generally they hunch down, "sulling," facing away. I saw him bring a hybrid back and maneuver it into the netting of a holding cage, supplying a pan of water before he went to lunch. The coyote dipped its chin into the water to verify that it really was going to be permitted to drink, then held its head away from the pan until we left. He shoots these, saving the skull and skin and looking for any telltale vestiges, such as the placement of a certain vein on the rear ankle that red wolves bequeathed to the hybrids which neither gray wolves nor coyotes quite duplicate, or perhaps some feathers on the forelegs inherited from a stray bird dog. Or he may discover a coyote's little teeth set into a wolf's lanky jaw. The wear on the incisors will show its approximate age. Wolves have more forehead in their skulls than a coyote, and grays have more than reds, but dogs, which are dish-faced, have more fore-head than wolves. Wolves boast big wide cheeks, big teeth and a proportionately lengthier, narrower braincase than coyotes or dogs, and the sagittal crest along the ridge of the skull where their powerful jaw muscles attach is more pronounced, but a dog's crest is higher than a coy-ote's. Coyotes, though, like wolves, have more space pro-vided within the margins of the skull for their hearing organs than dogs do.

Wolves' hind legs usually swing in the same line as their forelegs—they single-foot, as foxes do—whereas dogs put their hind feet between the prints of their front feet and show a shorter stride. With his tape measure for checking tracks and a siren for censusing, Riley goes

about looking at the feet of wolf-chewed calves to see if
they had ever really walked or were born dead. If something did kill them, he sees whether they were pulled
down by the ears, dog-style, or by the belly and the hams,
as a proper wolf would. Everywhere he stops his truck to
look at tracks—at the short feet of feral mongrels dumped
sick originally from hurrying cars along the Interstate, at
the wide feet of "duck dogs" lost during hunting season,
and the big heelpad and long foot of a true wolf. For the
record, too, he collects skulls and skins "off the fence,"
wherever the ranchers are still poisoning. When he
catches notable beasts that please him—two black coyotes that I saw, for instance—he "transplants" them.

"You transplanted them to heaven?" I asked.

"No, no, somewhere that they're going to be real
happy."

2

Texas encompasses considerably less state-owned park
and recreation land than New Jersey, and for its size,
remarkably little federal acreage too, because one of the
terms of its annexation to the United States was that the
federal government acquired no public domain. Its history
has been all private enterprise, and whereas Florida and
Southern California have fetishized their sunshine, Texas
has promoted the notion of space. Conservation legislation
of any kind has had a difficult time making much headway,

and many a landowner profits more from selling his deer to the hunters, at $250 per season per man, than from his cattle. Minnesota's wolves range mainly on government land, but Texas's live on private property, which means that their fate is tied to the inheritance tax and the local tax rate on land. If the ranching oligarchies fare badly, if their oil runs out or the assessors decide to put the squeeze on them in favor of new industry or summer development, or if a younger generation, coming into possession of the key spreads of property, wants to be rich in money instead of open spaces and maybe live elsewhere, it will spell the end of the red wolves.

In 1803 the U.S. purchase of Louisiana brought Anglo-American settlers to the eastern border of what is Texas. In 1821 Mexico gained her independence from Spain and the first Anglo colonists received permission to cross the boundary and settle southward on the Brazos under a Spanish-type "emprasario" system, whereby one energetic, commanding man was given a land grant on which he undertook to establish upwards of two hundred families, exercising quasi-judicial authority over them. This was a different conception of how to do things from the homesteaders' democratic methods in the American Midwest farther north, but within fifteen years the population of Texas quintupled. By 1830 the government in Mexico City was trying to forbid new Anglo settlements, to restrict immigration to Catholics, and otherwise pinch off the fast-developing trade relations between these Protestant citizens and their former homeland in the States. The Texans' War of Independence followed in 1836, but the emprasario method of settlement continued, and by the time that Texas joined the Union in 1845, the population had again quintupled, to nearly a hundred and fifty thousand.

Thus Texas was annexed, but on its own say so—take us as we are—its land its booty, and fashioned in its infancy by Spanish-Mexican autocracy and in its adolescence by successful revolt and outlawry. In all the pulling and hauling there had been no Eastern-seaboard counseling, no older-brother leavening by Virginia and Massachusetts army generals who supervised the birth of other states, or by a moderating President and Congress in Washington. In quick order the Civil War began, in which Texas, a slave state, went with the South, deposing its elected governor, Sam Houston, who was a Unionist, in the process. More revolt, hard riding and bitterness through Reconstruction, until by the onset of the new century Texas's population had increased to three million, but the crest of settlement had included an embittered surge of Southern veterans—burnt-out families grappling for land to assuage their loss. The Mexicans had been bundled off or reduced to a serf class, the Indians done away with, the wildlife mostly extirpated, and in a pride-heavy, insular setting soon to be thoroughly lubricated with oil there was little influence to dampen the frontier swagger.

Booted boys and behatted giants fish from the boardwalk at Port Aransas, knifing the croakers that they catch with enthusiasm. Even Cokes look bigger in Texas; and eating habits remain Brobdingnagian, with funny consequences for the midriff. But in Odessa I went to a "rattlesnake roundup" advertised for the municipal coliseum, and found the entrance thronged with ticket holders. This seemed what I was after—the old Texas rite for ridding the calving range of snakes—except that the crowd turned out to be fans attending a rock concert. The "rattlesnake roundup" was way around in back inside an adjunct shed, with three cars parked at the door.

Texas is still a good place to be rich in. Money is the stamp of excellence, yet in the southeast sections a more rooted conservatism, involving the illusion of an old-family tradition, has been carried over from the states nearby. Since it is a conservatism essentially unburdened by the weight of tragic circumstance of the Old South, one needn't become a contortionist to imagine that this is indeed the good life. Part of a wolf-seeker's regimen is to visit these grand mansion houses, and everywhere he encounters gracious living in the form of magnolias and spacious acreage patrolled by black cowhands—peacocks, guinea hens and fancy breeds of goose strolling the grounds, ten-foot alligators in private pools, pet deer in live-oak groves festooned with trailing moss. Quail and mourning doves, mimosas, pecans, orange trees, big-kneed cypresses, four cars in the garage, cool patios with iron grillwork, long lawns, little lakes, and girls and their daddies—girls so pretty Daddy doesn't quite know what to do with them.

These men of good fortune—men like Joe Lagow of Anahuac, and R. E. Odom, who lives across the Sabine River from Texas in Louisiana—glanced at my Vermont license plates, New York face and gray husky, and talked to me with caution. Lagow is a short jaybird of a man who serves as county commissioner and on a number of committees, and with his in-laws owns twenty-six thousand acres of snow-goose, red-wolf country. When I called to him across his aviary to ask if he was Joe Lagow, he swung around agreeably and said, "Yes, I'm what's left of him." Odom is younger and more reticent, even a little feline and courtly, in the Louisiana manner. We had tea in his jewelbox of a house, served by his white foreman. With his mother he owns a matchless spread of land in what is called Gum Cove, a luscious loop of grazing ground a few feet above sea level, enclaved within the badlands of Cameron Parish and reachable only by ferry across the Intracoastal Canal.

The time is past when Southern ranchers can be bamboozled into a reflexive show of hospitality, and various of these men gave me to understand, with conscious irony, that they were conservationists because they were conservatives and it would only be when new views took command that the ecology of their grasslands would be disrupted—smiling as they said this because of course a visiting Northern journalist was likely to represent those views. Nevertheless, the parade of exotic scribblers and photographers whom the environmental vogue is bringing to the door has started them thinking that the wolves that den on their mesquite knolls may be among the perquisites of wealth here on the Gulf; they've told their cowhands to quit killing them. It's the little operator, leasing pasturage for forty cattle that he has his hopes pinned on, who is still likely to put out traps, and if his few hundred acres happen to lie athwart a wolf run,

148

it won't much matter how many thousands more stretch trap-free all around.

I went to Wolf Corner in Thompson, Texas, just beyond the Houston city line, where a trapper named Charlie Grisbee has nailed up as many as thirty wolves or hybrids at a time. Grisbee wasn't home, but on his starchy lawn a wooden wolf was chasing a wooden family of ducks. It was a suburban sort of house interfaced with stone, all spruce and neat, with blue Pullman curtains in the windows of the garage. I'd asked whether Charlie was married and people had said very much so; they didn't think his wife especially liked his trapping, but that it "went with Charlie." A single twenty-pound coyote was hanging on the rack at the corner of a field next to the highway—attenuated-looking, rotting, twitching in the strong wind off the Gulf, with its head and tail hacked off, its rain-stained, rabbity fur and rabbity legs no longer distinguishable as those of a predator. In the grass for yards around were tibias, scapulas and backbone scraps, along with dewberries and Indian paintbrush, but some developers had now got hold of the field. I picnicked on the porch of a preempted farmhouse with a veteran fig tree for shade and honeysuckle all about.

In Danbury, in Brazoria County, I talked to Andrew Moller, among other old wolfers. Though Brazoria didn't bounty scalps, some of the fellows would deep-freeze what they caught and cash them in elsewhere. Moller is ninety-one. His grandfather jumped ship from a German whaler and bought land on Chocolate Bayou for five cents an acre, unfortunately sold off later. Once he was safely born, his father and his uncle had taken off for an adventure of their own, riding down the coast to Mexico for a couple of months, wading their horses across the many rivers they encountered at the mouth. And "in nineteen and eleven" he, a chip off the same block, had treated himself to a thousand-mile wagon ride around Texas, before paying thirty-five dollars for sixty cows, which over the next forty years he husbanded into a herd of fifteen hundred cattle. A traveling man, he mostly rented pasture for them. He trucked them to the Davis Mountains in West Texas, and to two decommissioned army camps in Arkansas and Oklahoma—unexpected long-grass pasturages on easy terms which he had hit upon during his hunting trips— always "keeping at least a nigger hired." Once he bought a thousand mares at four dollars a head, all of them running wild—he had to catch them—but sold them for ten dollars a head to a bootlegger who pirated them across the Sabine to Louisiana undipped and uninspected. Two of his old hands visited him recently in Danbury. He fed them catfish "and never heard two niggers laugh so much."

Using Walker hounds and Trumbulls, Moller caught little wolves in the nineteenth century when he was little and big ones when he grew up, till the barbed-wire fences were strung. A coyote, like a fox, will dodge into thick brush, he says, but a wolf "leaves the country." To catch him you first have to convince him that you are going to by running him ten miles through the sage and salt grass without letup. "Run a V on him" with other riders until his hind end wobbles and he hasn't gained a yard and begins to despair; then it may take another five or ten miles. Or if they could drive one into the Gulf of Mexico, they would keep roping him while he bit the ropes in two, until at last they drowned him. To run the wolves, even without a kill, kept the packs busted into isolated pairs which were less troublesome to the cattle, and generally Moller would catch the pups at the family rendezvous each fall. Sometimes, though, a varmint hunter would shoot a calf by mistake as it rose up suddenly in the grass. He'd had a couple of hog dogs as a boy that would chase any pup they came across, and with these he began wolfing on Chocolate Bayou, where the Amoco oil refinery now stands. In "nineteen and two" he was helping a trapper friend trail the wolves that hobbled off dragging the trap behind them, except it got to be such fun that they quit trapping and simply ran the creatures—ran them into swimming water where Moller would strip and grab a club and manhandle the wolf out to where the dogs could throttle it. Or he might rope it, haul it home to the hog pen and feed it cracklings and offal until his wife complained about the stink.

Moller is a well-set-up individual with pink coloring, a long face, a big pair of ears and nose, and a mellow voice. In 1895 eighteen inches of snow fell and half his father's cattle died. They skinned two hundred hides that week that fetched a dollar a hide in Galveston, both working as dollar-a-day cowboys afterwards, his father eating alligator tails and getting a dollar apiece for their hides too. Or they would paddle down Chocolate Bayou with four deer carcasses, put them on the city boat and trade them for a sack of green coffee in Galveston. In 1900 a hurricane blew down the house and washed away half the people who lived in the area, he says; one husband and wife held hands, grabbed hold of some driftwood and floated for thirteen miles.

The game was so plentiful—from cranes to doves— that on their hunts sometimes they couldn't hear the hounds for all the birds hollering. Sometimes, too, there were so many wolves about that when they went out after geese they couldn't creep close to a pond where a flight had just landed before some wolf would bound into the water to see whether any cripples were in the bunch, putting them all to flight. Moller captured the spring pups by riding up on a sand knoll where a lot of wolf tracks converged and prancing his pony around until its hooves broke through into the den. Then, on the following day, he'd jump the gyp-wolf (mama) there, and the day after that the pop. Once at the South Texas Wolf Hunters Association meet at the King Ranch, the Mexican hands had butchered a beef and hung it up for everybody to help himself, and brought out horses—the members had only had to bring along their own saddles. They all painted numbers on their dogs to score them in the chase, and Moller and a buddy stayed out late hounding a wolf until at last the creature "set his bucket down." He was exhausted, so they roped him, whipped the dogs away, and tied his mouth and carried him back across a horse, and at the big bonfire slipped off the ropes and heaved him into the crowd of wolfers to start the hunt all over again.

The cowhands close to Houston are mostly black, not Mexican, as they are towards the Rio Grande, or white, as in the bulk of Texas. Slingshots, in the old journals, are known as "nigger-shooters," but since at least the work was manly in the old days, for some of them it may have been a tolerable sort of place to be a slave—alone on horseback hassling the cattle much of the day. It still would seem to add up to a better life than growing peanuts in Mississippi, although the shacks along the road look just as rickety as Mississippi's, and though many of the people one encounters have a peculiarly screwed-tight intensity to their faces—extraordinary faces that a traveler sees nowhere else in the United States—as if they had been scorched in a crucible, like black faces in Mississippi. Can it simply be the sun?

One morning I was chatting with a rancher who said he wanted to kill all the turkey buzzards in the sky as well as the red wolves. There are plenty of buzzards. We could count about fifteen standing about in the treetops and roosting on fence posts. Overnight the rain ditches had filled, the sky still smelled of rain, but as we visited, the sun broke through, lying at a cannon's angle, the kind of morning sun that made you answer to it, irradiating dead as well as living things. Greens bled into blues and reds, white was black and black was white: too much color and too bright. The wind, which had been chilly, began to heat. Then, in this incredible intensity of light, what the buzzards did, following some lead from an elder, was all at once to spread their wings, not in order to rise and fly, but holding them outflung to dry.

What we were witnessing was not unfamiliar. Everybody has seen pictures of a totem pole topped by a raven carved with its wings outstretched, the Earth's creator, according to the maker of the totem pole. Ravens are the buzzards of the North. What we were privy to—fifteen buzzards spread-eagled, metal-colored in a violent sun— would have transfixed an Indian of the Northwest, would have provided a whole life's ozone to a woodcarver, a vision any warrior would have died for, if in fact his excitement didn't render him invincible. Fifteen images of the Creator in a rising sun would have propelled a great chief into his manhood after walking naked for a month; except we have no divine signs now.

I had settled in Anahuac at a café-motel where the lady displayed her late husband's Yale diploma in the office as a talking point. She missed Arkansas, claimed it had been an awful mistake for them to have left Little Rock nineteen years before, and looked that Southern mixture of left-over hopefulness and untidy despondency—hard shoulders and forearms but vulnerable breasts and soft hands. She served a rueful menu of chicken-fried steaks and heavy catfish to lonely oil workers and roaming fishermen. I was discouraged, angry at the way the wolf project was on the back burner for everybody but Glynn Riley. In Washington there was a mixture of flutter and indifference—even to get information had required a personal visit—and over the years Texas's Parks and Wildlife Department has taken what might politely be described as a minimum of interest. (Their black bears were allowed to fall practically to the vanishing point before receiving partial protection.) The wolves' blood characteristics had been studied not at a Texas medical center but in Minneapolis, and in Houston itself the concern, if possible, was fainter yet. The director of the Museum of Natural History, Dr. Thomas Pulley, an influential man, was not so much uninformed about the wolves as agin 'em. He hadn't exhibited the handsome skins that Riley had sent him, and liked to take the long view, speaking of man's impact on the world as related to evolution like the glaciers, belittling the notion of interfering as "causey, like preserving mustangs." He seemed bankerly in manner, a small-city, big-fish iconoclast with the mocking cast of mind that often develops in isolation, rubbing up against mostly laymen. He said that when he and his friends hunt deer they see plenty of coyotes.

The Houston zoo director, a civil servant, was not as self-assured. He had no wolves and agreed with me that though the zoos in San Antonio and Oklahoma City did keep one or two, it was incongruous that the only propagation program in the nation was way off in Tacoma, Washington. He said that to construct a "wolf woods" would cost only about seven thousand dollars, but that to raise such a piddling sum among the multimillionaires of Houston would be difficult because controversial, and so his efforts on behalf of disappearing species were devoted to the St. Vincent's parrot and Galápagos tortoise.

Riley carries hurt wolves to a veterinarian friend, Dr. Buddy Long, in the town of Winnie. Long pins together any broken bones (wolves will tear off a splint), administers penicillin and distemper shots and worms them. He is a man who "likes old things," and is the angel of Riley's program, having sunk thousands of dollars of his own modest funds into the work. He has a scrunched-together, matter-of-fact face, the mouth creased for smiling, and propagandizes as he makes his rounds among the cattlemen, several of whom still trap but who will telephone him when they catch something, if they don't like the idea of inviting a government man to poke about their property. The animal is a sad sight, clinched into a clutch of traps, with its feet mauled. Whatever toes are left he tends, or if the wolf is dead, he leaves it soaking in a tub for whenever the scientific community gets around to wanting to know what a red wolf looked like under the skin. At the time of my visit he had no legal authority to keep wild animals, and when the wolves he treated were ambulatory not a zoo in the country was prepared to take them, and so one night he'd leave the door of the pen open.

Long is a bit older than Glynn Riley, well settled in one of those delicious marriages that are a pleasure to catch sight of, and, as luck would have it, has been bolstering to Glynn. Through studying blood parasites he had become interested in the wolves, and now kept captives of his own in a big breeding arena. White on the lips and chin, with broad cheeks, narrow noses, a pointed attention and that skittery bicycling gait—whirling, almost fluttering, away from me along the fence—they were still jazzed up from the courting season, when they had chased each other all over Chambers County. Unfortunately this same month or two coincides with the calving season in the region, so that the ranchers see more of the wolves when they least want to.

156

Long took me wolfing along Elm Bayou, East Bayou, Onion Bayou. A blue heron was eating baby alligators, though in a few weeks it might be summering in one of the suburbs of Chicago. The geese in their yapping thousands flew up from the fields around us; they would soon be on the tundra. Long said that skunks are thick, and that though a grown wolf would have enough sense to steer clear of a rabid skunk, a blundering pup might get bitten and carry the disease into the packs.

"Around here you can look farther and see less than anywhere in the world," he said. But we inspected the "swimming holes" where the stockmen swim their cattle across the Intracoastal Canal every fall, then in the spring again, bringing them back to higher ground. We saw the burros that they use to halter-break the yearling colts, tying colt and burro neck to neck. He spoke about the problems of a cow vet. "Sometimes they won't get well and sometimes they won't die." At the fence gates we found wolf tracks. Now that the fields were drying off for spring the baby rabbits were hopping from the nest, and the wolves had scattered off the levees to catch them. Long said that sometimes the wolves will run a ranch dog right through a screen door, and twenty cattle through a fence, and pass the house again that night, barking so as to rib the dog. When hunted, they will circle into a herd if no other cover is close, and hamper the men from getting a shot at them by sticking beside the cattle.

Among the many lice-chewed cattle we saw one fine high-horned bull with a long dewlap, ears that hung down at a steep angle, a hump big as a camel's and a penis like a rhino's. He was a pretty mouse color, all the prettier for being so dangerous-looking underneath that comely pelt. "That one would try to get in your back pocket with you," said Long as we negotiated the gate.

The only other strong ally of Riley's I was able to find in Texas was Hank Robison, who sells cigarette lighters and ballpoint pens in Houston. A lobbyist and crusader, he has worked to get the local bounties removed. He lives in a workingman's district, has gold in the front of his mouth, is self-educated and self-conscious about it, and financially must live by his wits, he says. But posters of lions and tigers stare off the walls of his small house; his blinds are dog-chewed. He talks like a dogged cross between a crank and social worker and is a fervid letter writer, keeping a file so that no officeholder can get away with not replying to him. He has a flatly single-minded fighter's face, taking you for where you stand, and when knocked down, obviously will not stay down, because his delight is just precisely to get up again. He camps in the Big Thicket on weekends and lives for his family as well as for wild animals, and yet in him I thought I saw what I notice in other enthusiasts and in myself: the injured man who recognizes in the running wolf his wounds.

Riley could comprehend a person preferring to live in the city if he liked going to the movies or had the money to eat in restaurants, but what he couldn't understand about the Eastern cities was the matter of muggers. Working with wolves, he wasn't afraid of muggers. "Why don't they clean them out of there?" Like Lynn Rogers in Minnesota, apparently he had a picture of himself walking down the avenues and, if he saw a mugger, punching him in the mouth. Of course, being familiar with firearms, he could adjust his image when I said that the mugger was likely to be armed, but he continued to presume that the solution lay in individual acts of heroism. What neither man could grasp was how *many* muggers there are.

Glynn has poisoned pocket gophers in East Texas and prairie dogs in West Texas, and out in Muleshoe in the Panhandle did rabbit counts for the Bureau, where he saw some odd spectacles: a badger and a coyote turning over cow chops in a partnership to eat the beetles underneath; an eagle snatching a duck from a windmill spillway. The eagles perched on the boxcars where feed was stored to spear the pack rats living underneath, and early one morning he watched a coyote filch a rabbit from an eagle, the coyote's chest fur shining nobly in the sun. Once in a while he'd drive a hundred miles or so to chat with an old wolfer who had shot the last gray Western lobos at their watering holes. One time the fellow had ridden here to the Gulf to dispose of a hog-killing red wolf: lay waiting for it behind the pen the night that he arrived, and when he heard the hog scream, shot the wolf, and the next day left —too many people here, not that big Western country. "We thought there'd always be another wolf. We didn't know they would ever play out," he told Glynn.

Riley's best thrill, when he has visited the study crew in Minnesota, has been to feel with his hands the outsized tracks the wolves make there in the fluffy snow. Gray wolves are real wolves in a way that red wolves aren't, and the black taiga wolves of the Yukon and the white

159

arctic wolves are larger still. Some day he hopes to have a hand in studies of them all: jaguars too. He's a predator man and he wants size—dire wolf, cave bear! Then, because he was a novice on snowshoes, he began to make strange tracks himself, falling down and flinging out his arms. For days it was the joke in camp: *that's* were Glynn Riley from Texas fell down, and *there's* where he fell down again.

Like old-time trapping, Riley's is a lonely business. His best friend lives six hundred miles away in the Trans-Pecos town of Marathon, Texas. He's a mountain-lion hunter whom I'll call Mike Marfa, and the two of them became acquainted at what Marfa likes to call "rat meetings," where the varmint-control technicians of the Fish and Wildlife Service get together to talk shop, mostly about killing rodents and rabbits. But these two were men who had a penchant for pulling down a bigger creature, and, beyond that, were outdoorsmen with a vocation for it (Marfa likes to say that he's already caught enough coyotes to fill ten diesel trucks). When the two of them do manage a visit they can hardly contain their pleasure. They open the pungent brown bottles that Riley sets such store by, bobbing their heads like connoisseurs above the beaver oil and bobcat urine, two years in the brewing, though Marfa likes to tease Riley that it is where you put the trap, not so much what you sprinkle on it, that does the job.

Marfa is another man who knows more than many of the professors do who hold Chairs on the strength of their investigations into ethology, and sometimes comes back snorting from the symposia he goes to, saying he'd like to hear from the guy who *catches* their lions for them. For years he was the state's principal lion hunter, when the Bureau had a hundred and fifty trappers giving the coyotes a going-over. He was paid a little more and got up earlier too, he likes to claim, kidding Riley, and went out on muleback the whole day long, chasing after his hounds, instead of tooling about in a pickup truck like Riley and the rest, to prune the lions back to the edges of Big Bend National Park from a line which corresponded more or less to U.S. Highway 90. When I first met him he was on his way home from an excursion to Florida where he had demonstrated for the World Wildlife Fund that the Florida panther was rarer than Florida's wildlife officials had believed. His pack of mottled Walker hounds—a home brew he has bred and culled and whittled on over the years, and doesn't sell or swap or loan, he says, any more than a carpenter would his tools—were sleeping in a fresh pile of hay in the back of his truck, so placid after traveling so far that they spoke well for him. He and Riley took them for a run after bobcat along a bayou bank, but then, although Riley was eager to have him stay overnight and go to the Houston Fat Stock Show, which happened to be on that week, and although he himself was wistful about the possibility too, he said he had another twelve hours of driving ahead and didn't want to keep the dogs cooped up any longer than that. He's the type who scoops up every hitchhiker on the road, otherwise stopping nowhere, but compared to Riley, his mannerisms are gruff and harsh, and he is proud of going all day in the Big

Bend desert without either water or food. Like so many other wildlife men, he was not in the Marines when he was a youngster and probably should have been. Where the bear man, Lynn Rogers, had made the burler's leap to city living in Minneapolis in the winter, Riley and Marfa had not. Riley had relinquished much of his hunter's spark, however, to a reflective attitude that suited his present work, but Marfa, whom Riley rather looks up to, was just as hot as ever; he had quit the Bureau and when he wasn't working on an experimental program to transplant mountain lions from the Big Bend country to South Texas, supported himself as a private lion hunter in the Big Bend region, and by trapping the last few lobo wolves down in the Mexican states of Durango and Chihuahua.

Marfa let me delve about with him a bit in his own territory, first wanting and then deciding that he didn't want a full-dress magazine article written about himself, but through both men I caught a sense of the cycle of wolf and coyote hunting.

The coyote is of course the "barking wolf," the Trickster of so many Indian tribes—a deity to the Chinooks and the Navajos, a subtle animal with a taste for the suckled milk in a lamb's stomach, for instance, which the simpler-minded bobcat does not share—the New World version of the jackal, and yet a creature so highly thought of that the pregnant women of certain Indian tribes would wear its testicles next to their stomachs to ward off difficulties. The fall is nonetheless the season when the guileless pups are dashing around; it is a chance to wipe out the year's crop while they are wet behind the ears, and was the season for the getter-gun until the getter-gun as a device was disallowed. Any witches' brew could be used to bait the knob—possum juice, rotted gopher, dead rattlesnake or frog—and since the pup took eight or ten leaps to die, more of the hunter's time was consumed in locating its little corpse in the brush than in any other part of the job.

In the winter the getters weren't as effective and the sort of guy without any particular skill who had coasted along in the fall by putting out a lot of them took a back seat to the serious trapper. Winter is the mating season, and the emphasis is on catching the adults as they hustle about, pissing at scenting stations and trailing one another. Sex is what interests them, not picking up the quaint and curious scents that getter-guns are baited with. The trapper, milking the bladders, cutting the musky anal glands out of the specimens he bags, creates some scent posts of his own or activates others—a turkey wing lying next to a sheep path—that the smarter coyotes will step up to. In a bog in Anahuac, the fellow might set his trap at the end of a footlog, with a wad of moss under the pan so that a raccoon's weight won't depress it.

In the spring and summer the animals lose interest in everything except their pups, and travel in a beeline between the den and hunting grounds. Trotting back full-bellied from a long drink at a spring, they may stop for a moment and piddle at the turkey wing or even investigate the outré smells on the bait knob of a "getter," but generally this is when the professionals hunt for dens. Den-hunting is a specialty, intuitive, distinct. The steel-trap men are condescending about the cyanide go-getter—a kind of scatter-shot method, a glib, perfunctory tool—and yet compared with trapping, den-hunting is downright purist and arcane. It's catching the animals alive, by hand, in their hidden home, and some predator hunters hardly bother to trap at all, killing a presentable quota of coyotes just by finding and digging up the year's new dens. Usually they ride, because a coyote fears a man on horseback somewhat less, and what the hunter looks for is a bustling hodge-podge of tracks that, as he studies them, begin to offer evidence of radiating from a given point which the coyotes have tried to conceal. Often the den faces southeast from a slight elevation, and he may try to call one of the parents toward him with a "squeaker" made from a piece of a cow's horn which emits a rabbit's squeal. If, having dismounted, he sees the coyote first and holds his fire until it scents him, he will have the benefit of its last quick anxious glance in the direction of the den to guide him on, before it takes evasive action. If the grownups attempt to decoy him he shoots them, then looks sharp for the first pup, which will streak for the hole as soon as it sights him. He tumbles about in the brush, grabbing the pups and clubbing them, or if they are very young he must dig, hooking them out from underground with a wire prong twisted on the end. If either parent has escaped him, he will bury a dead whelp with one foot exposed and set traps alongside it and by the den.

In sheep territory the javelinas root holes under the woven fences that coyotes also make use of, and this is where the ancient craft of snaring can be practiced. Then, by contrast, there are hunters who are primarily marksmen and shoot the creatures from a helicopter. But none of these systems will suffice after the less vigilant 70 percent of the population has been eliminated. There are always a few coyotes which flatten down instead of bolting when the helicopter makes its pass over the chaparral, and which keep their pups clear of the getter-guns. For these holdouts some studying is necessary; the animal becomes individualized, and a Riley or a Marfa becomes interested. Or they may meet an animal like Adolph Murie's blithe classic coyote in the valley of the Yellowstone which trotted toward him carrying a sprig of sagebrush in its jaws that it tossed up and caught and tossed and caught. *

When the Fish and Wildlife Service supervisors in San Antonio decided that the Big Bend mountain lions had had enough pruning, they set Marfa on a series of eccentric research labors, such as catching sixty coyote puppies "by Friday" for a sex-ratio study, collecting adults for a test of poisons, or gathering coyote urine and red-wolf skulls. (The number of red wolves killed in order to verify their existence as a species and then to train successive research cadres must surpass the number so far "saved.") Finally Marfa went into business for himself, charging the sheep ranchers $250 per lion, and more for the Sierra Madre lobos he has been capturing in Durango lately, working for the stockmen's association there. In some respects a wolf is more vulnerable than a coyote, because of the com-

* Murie, *Ecology of the Coyote in the Yellowstone* (Washington, D.C.: National Park Service, Fauna Series Number 4, 1940), p. 38.

plexity of its social life and because it is bolder and therefore more accessible, but since it travels farther, in another way it is less so. These are "named" wolves, the last
of their kind in an enormous spread of territory, in their
way almost as endangered as Riley's wolves are, and correspond to the famous "outlaw" wolves of the American
Great Plains a half a century ago. Like them, they're
quirky, lonely, queer, atypical beasts, final survivors because they have allowed themselves only the sparsest
pleasures. Marfa carries a handful of traps as he rides his
mule around for a period of days or weeks to spy out
some small chink in the precautionary tactics of the wolf
he is after—some stray indulgence by which it still tries
to amuse itself that has escaped the notice of all the
other trappers who have had a go at it. These Mexican
lobos have short pretty heads, and you must know the
length of the neck and stride in situating the trap.

One such wolf, "Las Margaritas," took him eleven
months to catch, humbling him, he says, and in the meantime, it was claimed, slaughtering ninety-six cattle on a
single large ranch nearby. The only entertainment left
"Margaret" after so many narrow escapes in a lengthy
career was killing steers, once she was safely inside a
pasture. She was poison-proof because she fed at her own
kills and nowhere else, and never a second time at one
of them. Already missing two front toes, she would follow
a different route coming and going. If she arrived on a
logging road, she exited by way of a cattle track; if through
a canyon, by a high pass. She avoided other wolves, although from loneliness she sometimes would howl behind

the ranchers' barns. She would not go close to the message stations of other wolves, but instead would squat wistfully to make her mark at a safe distance, so that he could not catch her by the ordinary technique of setting a trap at a scent post or manufacturing a bogus station with the urine of a foreign wolf. Some outlaws, he says, entirely give up trying to communicate with other wolves and use only their own scenting stations. Once, indeed, she did step in one of his traps, but the hole carved into her foot by the two toes that she was missing happened to fit across the pan and saved her. She jumped for her life.

She traveled continually, having been hunted with hounds often after a meal, and there was no predicting where she would go. Over the years, hundreds of traps had simply been left blind for her in paths across the mountainsides she ranged, which gradually had lost their human smell and any surface scars to show the ground had been worked on. But some of them had become bone-yards for other animals that had been caught instead, and the rest she avoided by her spartan custom of stepping mostly on the rocks and stones, or else on ground too hard to dig in without leaving a permanent sign. On the road, if there was any indication that a rider had dismounted or that a man had left his truck, even the day before, she immediately veered off, not waiting to discover what he might have been up to. Without the fellowship of a pack, with nowhere safe enough for her to go to relax except among the actual cattle herds, killing was her life and her relations with her pursuers her only intimacy, so when at last Marfa did catch her—when he had almost given up—it was in a trap that he had left blind some weeks before next to a corral she liked to hang about. She pulled the stake out of the ground and painfully dragged the trap as far as she could, but all the ranch hands turned out to chase her down. Only then was it revealed that notorious "Margaret," so security-ridden that she squatted meekly to piss like a bitch, all along had been a male.

When this methodical search had palled, Marfa dashed off behind his light little slipping lion hounds—skinny so their feet hold up and so they can twist through the canyon cracks and into any boulder pile (for which he has a "climbing dog")—to run down one of the infrequent lions left. He sight-trailed for the pack over the alkali ground, where the scent, as dry as smoke, had blown away. Where there were grass and sticks again they'd pick it up. Salt blocks, windmills and fencing are what makes ranching here. Durango is also the starving country where wetbacks come from, and any deer whose prints show up is tracked relentlessly. There are human outlaws in the Sierra Madre as well, and Marfa, lean from his regimen of two meals shoveled in twelve hours apart, living very nearly on a level with a lion, with the two expressions that his face falls into—boyish and bleak—went about with his rifle handy and his bedroll and mule and dogs.

Another noteworthy wolf he caught because his dogs showed him its single small inabstinence. It liked to go up on top of a mesa to a water tank with an earthen dam and wallow in that one soft place on a long-dead skunk lying in sweet-smelling grass. He captured a wolf called Wide Gait using a month-old turd which he had saved from its former ladylove, whose Spanish name was Nearly Black and whom he had trapped previously with an old turtle shell. "Dead as a hammer," he says.

Turds represent survival in the desert or the woods and are beloved by animals for that: a meal put to use, the gift of life. Of a woodsman, too, you'll hear it said, "He was the best deer-hunter that ever took a shit in the woods." Marfa showed me how to distinguish a ringtail's scats (small-bore, on top of a rock, containing scorpion pincers and tails) from a raccoon's; a kit fox's fuzzy-toed, dainty prints from a gray fox's; and trundled me about, pointing out abundant lion scrapes in the sandy canyons we explored next to the Rio Grande. Lions scratch with their forefeet for their feces and their hind feet for urine, partly hiding the first but ballyhooing the latter. Their front feet make a bigger, rounder print, so people sometimes think one track is two.

This is country where one finds the arrows wetbacks put together in the dry streambeds with stones—where once in the Christmas Mountains Marfa found the skeleton of a "wet" who had gotten himself lost. He pointed out a mountain in Coahuila, a twelve-hour walk up a canyon tributary to the Rio Grande, which has a cave so big a plane could fly into its mouth, and cool high pine forests where a few black bears are still holding out. He spoke about another sanctuary, in Chihuahua, where until recently all the American cats could be found—jaguarundis, ocelots, bobcats, lions and jaguars—though now every such shangri-la in Mexico is shrinking faster than a puddle on hot city pavement. The last of the grizzly bears, he says, was blown up with nitroglycerin wired to a honey-smeared log.

An ocelot leaves more scent than a bobcat and doesn't fight the dogs as hard; a jaguarundi is lithest in the thickets and the toughest to trail, he said. Lions and lobos are a force, a *frequency*, if you will: once maybe the trombone, now the oboe in the orchestra. They are the Headless Horseman who, once he is gone, exists only in fairy tales, and although most of us can get along without hearing the oboe's note or seeing the Headless Horseman ride, in Riley and Marfa I had come close to locating the people who can't. Marfa, in particular, who has hunted jaguars in the jungle in Campeche too, talks about retiring to British Honduras, where in the wet woods he envisions the cats forever plentiful, leaving a trail for his dogs "as strong as a garbage truck." In the desert in the early morning he lets the vultures be his guide and trucks his dogs to where they are. Then, with the water *tinajas* fifteen or twenty miles apart, he gets his lion.

Red wolves howl in a higher, less emotive pitch than gray wolves and don't blend with each other quite as stylishly, though they do employ more nuances and personality than a coyote family's gabble. A coyote's howl sounds hysterical, amateurish by comparison, chopped and frantic, almost like barnyard cackling, or, in an early description, "like a prolonged howl the animal lets out and then runs after and bites into small pieces." The only likely-looking wolves I actually saw during my several visits were two smashed dead on the highway, which I passed at high speed as I was leaving Texas. They were red, sizable and somber, at least from the perspective I had by then accumulated. They were probably mates, the second having lingered alongside the first, and now were angled affectionately rump to rump—the copulative position—in death.

Once, too, alone one night along Elm Bayou, I howled up a wolf a quarter of a mile away that sounded querulous and yowly, variable and female. We were beginning to converse, but I left it to answer another wolf howling a mile beyond. This wolf and I talked back and forth, until I started to wonder. The sound jerked and creaked too unsteadily for a wolf and yet was pitched too low to be a coyote, and wasn't barky enough for a feral dog—almost like a windmill. In fact, that's what it was; I'd left a real wolf for a windmill.

In these inquiries I had begun to glimpse the noble stretch of science when it grabs hold of a sea of data and persuades it to jell. In a still-primitive, ambiguously motivated backwater area of scholarship there was nevertheless a majesty to the picture as it emerged. Predators are smarter than herbivores, usually need to sleep more, and possess the invaluable ability to vomit, and when the findings on these biggest beasts are combined, one understands better the grizzly with its "attack distance" developed for a life on the plains, the black bear thriving by gourmand eating and a love of holes, the mountain lion avoiding competition and starvation by avoiding wolf country and its own kind, the wolf avoiding competition and starvation by a hierarchal social existence. Unluckily, the very means of population control that had enabled each

171

of them to prosper while ruling the roost—the graphic social life, in some cases, and the slow, problematical birth rate of more solitary creatures such as bears or eagles—is now depleting them. These discoveries were being made, on the one hand, by scholars many of whom might have been laughed out of the lab if they had been working in another branch of science, and on the other, by observers in the field whose woodsmanship was only a faint shadow of that of the centuries when the wilderness (and these animals) were real. But I'd met men who wouldn't have done badly in any era of woodsmanship.

THAT GORGEOUS
GREAT NOVELIST

There is an old pernicious sentiment in circulation, which I see posted up in government bureaus no less than commune kitchens, as if its time had come around once again. "None of us is as smart as all of us," the placards proclaim—a depressing thought, referring not to political democracy, of course, but to the committee mind. The best retort has always been to point to a genius, especially an artistic genius, which is one of the reasons why it is so salutary to have a few of them around. When the fellow's achievements pass a certain point, they become achievements held in common, much more than if it really were true that "none of us is as smart as all of us." We can leave him to his alcoholism or old-man's sense of failure, if that's how it works out for him, and absorb what he painted or wrote as our own. Don Quixote, Huck Finn, even Dreiser's Hurstwood, are figures that were contained in everybody from the beginning, but more so after they had been set down.

And the health of any branch of the arts depends somewhat on the existence within it of a heavyweight or two, a Picasso, a champion who, no matter how far away he may be geographically or in technique or spirit, does every practitioner good. In fact, the absence of just such a robustly gifted novelist, inspiriting the writers, exciting the readers, may have more to do right now with the malaise felt by many novelists than all the theories of form which make up what Henry James once called "the periodical prattle about the future of fiction." Since *his* triumph would spread out like the coattails of a statesman to give everybody else a big boost, it's hardly more pleasant for the rest of us to resign ourselves to the lack of a literary genius on the horizon than it is to settle, on a personal level, for hopes that have become merely lively, not exalted.

Maybe I have rabbit ears, but I've been hearing the phrase "minor novelist" a lot lately. Generally an editor rather than a writer says it, mentioning some fairly respectable name from the recent past—good enough and lucky enough to be remembered, at least—and I ask myself whether there really is a "major" and "minor," then admit that I suppose there is. Not that it's a distinction worth repeating so frequently, but everybody should recognize his limitations at some point in order to make the best of his talents, not wasting too many days imagining that he is Dickens, but buckling down to write his Alexandrian *Justine*. Like turning forty, this natural watershed may be anticipated so feverishly that when it arrives the transition is painless. The man simply stops looking forward exclusively; he thinks for a moment, so far what have I done?

One starts reading about one's classmates in the newspaper, friends high in the Interior Department or the Metropolitan Museum of Art. Guys once fat and shy are now fat, funny and influential. They breeze through Kennedy Airport, and their teenagers meet them. One chap is in the news for contributing one million dollars to President Nixon's hidden campaign fund in individual $3,000 checks, but I know him well because at prep school we were assigned to the same corridor—a collection of people regarded as incorrigible maladroits and known informally as The Zoo. Still another joker, from a famously rich family usually expert at eluding interviewers, has fallen into a messy bankruptcy and spilled his guts to the first girl reporter who drove up the long driveway and rang his doorbell. His wife, one reads, dashed from the back of the house, made a rush at the girl and drove her off, but not before the reporter had sensed, in that couple of minutes, the whole story, both of the business fiasco and the hash that their marriage was now.

These men have grown up, for better or worse. So have the editors who roll the words "minor novelist" on their tongues, and although it makes me uneasy to have their eyes fixed on me, possibly they're thinking of writers they publish, or of their own literary hopes when they were young. Journalism is in fine shape—straight, first-class, rough-washcloth journalism—but beyond immersing ourselves in the books admiringly, we don't know quite how to take that fact, literature before having generally been some variety of *make-believe*. While it's true that the journalists who write about subjects other than poverty and war sometimes do fictional journalism, like the rough-washcloth journalists they're human too, by no means ten feet tall. One has the feeling that they're right in believing the distinctions between fiction and nonfiction have blurred and begun to dissolve, but that they have yet to strike the right road.

The essay is a vulnerable form. Rooted in middle-class civility, it presupposes not only that the essayist himself be demonstrably sane, but that his readers also operate upon a set of widely held assumptions. Fiction can be hallucinatory if it wishes, and journalism impassive, and so each continues through thick and thin, but essays presuppose a certain standard of education in the reader, a world ruled by some sort of order—where government is constitutional, or at least monarchical, perhaps where sex hasn't wandered too far from its home base and religion isn't so smothering that nobody knows where babies come from—where people seek not fragmentation but a common bond.

Part of what made a man civilized used to be that he could distinguish between what was funny and what was not. Now so much is funny that the question has been pushed beyond that to whether he can pick out what is part of civilization and what is not. People seem to be engaged in delaying actions of various kinds—resisting getting divorced, resisting chucking over everything. The prescience of Ionesco's play *Rhinoceros* may be that we will begin to see our acquaintances knock themselves off. Though novels also have traditionally been written for the sensibility of the middle class—people who were willing to begin by agreeing on what that is—there is a majesty to fiction, ringing back to the itinerant storyteller who went everywhere and enthralled everyone, by means of puppets or the sterling motions of his hands, even if his audience didn't speak the same language he did. Whether fiction is told with words or by the hands casting shadows on a screen or through the intervention of a movie camera, its classlessness, as good as gold, can survive anything.

In Victorian biographies we read that "Although Mr. Morewarrant's formal schooling was sketchy, he had the run of his grandfather's extensive library at home." Perhaps that's a way to think of the permanent body of literature: a rambling library with ladders to reach all the shelves. Ingmar Bergman's movies would belong there, but as far as I am aware, only one authentically great book has been published in the past fifteen years. It's a novel, *One Hundred Years of Solitude*, by the Columbian, Gabriel Garcia Marquez; and the eagerness with which so many people have hailed it (as well as, lately, Thomas Pynchon's *Gravity's Rainbow* and E. L. Doctorow's *Ragtime*, which are surely authentic attempts) indicates, first of all, how they've pined for a great book to hail, and secondly, that if another fixture of world literature had appeared we probably would have heard about it.

I assume that we do know who our flagship writers are. In the United States so far, among people around forty with much work behind them, we can take them to be John Updike and Philip Roth. Both are so good, so various and have written so much that they can't help but be underrated, reviewing by its nature being a random, carping affair. Each is touching as well as impressive: Updike for writing about twenty years of marriage while everybody else was writing about twenty years of divorce, and for trying hard to be a broad-spectrum writer at an unlikely time; Roth because of the intensity of his commitment to individual intuitions and the daring of individual books. I was a classmate of Updike's and saw him write the *Lampoon* single-handed, then (almost) *The New Yorker*, and from ignoble jealousy didn't manage to read him until about ten years ago. When I did, I was stunned by how marvelous he was. Suddenly in an exact contemporary I saw dimensions bigger than mine, saw what I hadn't done well in my own books, or had scarcely attempted to do. If writing is long-distance running, then I had in front of me a pacer who was extraordinary and would stretch my legs while gaining all the time. Roth, for some reason, I've never felt envious of. For one thing, he wasn't a classmate; for another, he was a creature of impulse like me, and I felt much in common with him, though, like Updike, he was a revelation and had outstripped me in what he'd attempted.

But since these two were ahead of me, I wanted them to spurt way out in front, to write the big books redefining, reaffirming the indispensability of literature, to be the big fish whose swimming feats would glorify us all. And with the best will in the world, so far they've been

178

unable to. One reason why we are fond of Norman Mailer and forgive his high jinks is that he has worn his heart on his sleeve in this regard. His books, taken together, may not be as good as Saul Bellow's, but his ambition as well as his talent has been mountainous and his boyish weight-lifting appealing. We're longing to cheer on a gorgeous great novelist, and the point about Mailer is that, almost alone among the good writers, for instance, he recognized that the moon shots were a monumental occasion, an event that would change civilization, and set out, just as he had during World War II and the political upheavals between, to get the scene down.

You don't find warmed-over Hemingway in Mailer, or second-rate Bellow in Roth, or cut-rate Nabokov in Updike. Mailer is more intelligent than Hemingway and mixes a richer verbal brew. Updike is a wider thinker than Nabokov, less flawed by the strange, cold-fish vices of his emigré maître. Roth, without losing any of the generous spirits that mark Bellow's fiction, is more single-minded and intense. But are they better than Hemingway, Nabokov, Bellow? The answer would have to be no. Two range out wider than their predecessors and consequently fall short and lose focus, by comparison; the third is narrower in joining himself to the issues and thus less absorbing. And it is our loss.

We look to the mysterious Mr. Pynchon, or Joyce Carol Oates. They too work and wait—we all work and wait—but the masterpieces don't come. Maybe it will take the energy of the new continents, the new century. More likely not: just a longer wait. In the meantime we look

179

at Faulkner on our shelves and are glad that our lives overlapped for a little with his. Eight thousand people a year visit Faulkner's white, dense-as-a-diamond little house in its cedar grove in Oxford, Mississippi. The upstairs and east side of the downstairs were his wife's, but the west side of the downstairs—two rooms and a hall—was his. There is a small spartan bed and a tiny writing desk built out from the wall like a shelf, with just enough space for his elbows and an Underwood. The books are a miscellany that other authors had sent, the paintings are his mother's, the view is whatever scraps of field can be seen beyond the carport. The lean old Negro who showed me around said that Faulkner "lived a peculiar life . . . a world of his own . . . All he did was write."

CITY

WALKING

There is a time of life some-
where between the sullen fugues of adolescence and the
retrenchments of middle age when human nature becomes
so absolutely absorbing one wants to be in the city constantly, even at the height of the summer—Nature can't
seem to hold a candle to it. One gobbles the blocks, and
if the weather is sweaty, so much the better; it brings
everybody else out too. To the enthusiast's eye, what
might later look to be human avarice is simply energy,
brutality is strength, ambition is not wearisome or repel-
lent or even alarming. In my own case, aiming to be a
writer, I knew that every mile I walked, the better writer
I'd be; and I went to 20th Street and the Hudson River
to smell the yeasty redolence of the Nabisco factory, and
to West 12th Street to sniff the police stables. In the meat
market district nearby, if a tyro complained that his back
ached, the saying was, "Don't bleed on me!"

Down close to the Battery the banana boats used to
unload (now they are processed in Albany). Banana boats

were the very definition of seagoing grubbiness, but bejeweled snakes could be discovered aboard which had arrived from the tropics as stowaways. On Bleecker Street you could get a dozen clams on the half shell for fifty cents if you ate them outdoors; and on Avenue A, piroshki, kielbasa and suchlike. Kids still swam from piers west of the theater district in the Hudson and under Brooklyn Bridge, and I was on the lookout among them for Huckleberry Finn. He was there, all right, diving in, then scrambling up a piling, spitting water because he hadn't quite learned how to swim. In the evening I saw him again on Delancey Street, caught by the ear by a storekeeper for pilfering.

Oh yes, oh yes! one says, revisiting these old walking neighborhoods. Yorkville, Inwood, Columbus Avenue. Our New York sky is not muscular with cloud formations as is San Francisco's, or as green-smelling as London's, and rounding a corner here, one doesn't stop stock-still to gaze at the buildings as in Venice. The bartenders like to boast that in this city we have "the best and worst," yet intelligent conversation, for example, is mostly ad-libbed and comes in fits and starts, anywhere or nowhere; one cannot trot out of an evening and go looking for it. We have our famous New York energy instead, as well as its reverse, which is the keening misery, the special New York craziness, as if every thirteenth person standing on the street is wearing a gauzy hospital smock and paper shower slippers.

Edmund G. Love wrote a good city walker's book some years ago called *Subways Are for Sleeping*. Indeed they

were, but now if the transit police didn't prevent old bums
from snoozing the night away while rumbling back and
forth from Brooklyn to the Bronx, somebody would set
them on fire. Up on the street hunting parties are abroad,
whom the walker must take cognizance of; it's not enough
to have your historical guidebook and go maundering
about to the Old Merchant's House on East 4th Street.
A pair of bravos will ask you for a light and want a light;
another pair, when your hands are in your pockets, will
slug you. If you're lucky they will slug you; the old bar
fighters complain about how risky fighting has become.
You must have a considerable feel for these things, an
extra sense, eyes in the back of your head: or call it a
walker's *emotional range*. You must know when a pistol
pointed at you playfully by a ten-year-old is a cap pistol
and when it's not; whether someone coming toward you
with a broken bottle is really going for you or not. We
have grown to be students of police work—watching a
bank robber scram as the squad cars converge, watching
a burglar tackled, watching four hoodlums unmercifully
beating a cop until four patrol cars scream to a halt and
eight policemen club down the hoods.

Nevertheless, if you ask people who have some choice
in the matter why they live in a particular neighborhood,
one answer they will give is that they "like to walk." Walking is a universal form of exercise, not age-oriented or
bound to any national heritage, and costs and implies
nothing except maybe a tolerant heart. Like other sports,
it calls for a good eye as well as cheerful legs—those
chunky gluteus muscles that are the butt of mankind's

oldest jokes—because the rhythm of walking is in the sights and one's response as much as simply in how one steps. In America at the moment it may seem like something of a reader's or an individualist's sport, because we are becoming suburban, and the suburbs have not adjusted to the avocation of walking yet. But they will.

And yet times do change. Only this spring I was in a river town on the Mississippi, loafing on a dock the barges tie to, on the lookout for Huckleberry Finn once again. He was there, all right, with a barefoot, red-headed, tow-headed gang. They had sandy freckles and wore torn pants; Miss Watson still cut their hair. They were carrying a pailful of red-eared turtles and green frogs from the borrow pit behind the levee, and were boasting about the garfish they had noosed with a piece of piano wire. They began daring each other, and what the dare turned out to be—the best they could think of—was which of them had nerve enough to reach down and taste the Mississippi!

Now, muggers are herd creatures like the rest of us; they too have a "rush hour." So if a walker is indeed an individualist there is nowhere he can't go at dawn and not many places he can't go at noon. But just as it demeans life to live alongside a great river you can no longer swim in or drink from, to be crowded into the safer areas and hours takes much of the gloss off walking—one sport you shouldn't have to reserve a time and a court for.

WHERE

THE

ACTION IS

Nearly forty years ago Cyril Connolly, in his memoir of the same title, cited journalism as one of the chief "enemies of promise" which a young writer ought to steer clear of. Although the magazine hackwork and book reviewing he was particularly referring to does remain a rather unfruitful endeavor, it is unlikely that he or any other observer could so crisply dismiss journalism now. Any number of first books by eely, quick and yet encompassing new talents would refute the idea. If a tug-of-war were waged between the young and serious novelists round about and the serious young journalists, the latter might well win, both with respect to giftedness and numbers. They are beset with opportunities—up to the Adam's apple in opportunities— perhaps even including the possibility of "accomplishing something." Journalism itself in fact is the theater of operations toward which a literary youngster who still believes in the American dream would naturally incline—where it might appear to him that if he tackles a large project

185

and works hard at it he can become rich and famous, though he may be writing about some aspect of the overall destruction of the American dream. (Novelists get rich too, but by a much more whimsical process.)

We may wince a bit, watching some of the journalists of a political temperament who hobnob incessantly with the useful or the mighty, cultivating one fellow, dropping another, as chameleonlike and power-conscious as any congressman. At a party they flush sexually if a newsmaker enters the room, and bring to mind the maxim which is also applied to policemen, that "it takes a thief to catch a thief." This is seldom really true of the police, or of journalists either, for that matter. Indeed, it's probably unfair to allow he-man novelists their traditional palship with boxers, bookies, prostitutes and other violent or ambiguous types, while frowning on the mesmerism which worldlier men of power exercise on the sort of journalist who has "a nose for news." There is more difficulty than this moral factor for journalism as a vehicle for talent accompanying the tilt built into it of keeping *up-to-date*. The individual needn't go whole hog like a newspaperman—on top of, embodying, everybody else's point of view. Unless he resists, the pressures of his profession nevertheless are going to push him into typifying in his own course of inquiry the twists and bias of his day.

But if even a first-rate journalist runs the risk of becoming a weathervane, the temptation of the earnest novelist is "posterity." He can look to posterity for a verdict on his work if he doesn't like what's come his way so far, until the danger is that in the meantime he may close his ears.

186

What has happened, however, which has so stunned novelists, is that for the first time since novel-writing began they have no assurance that there will be a posterity to set the record straight. This absence of a future to look to—a time of solace or of reckoning—has flummoxed plenty of other people (for example, husbands, wives) who are engaged in improbably long-term commitments too.

The task of explaining ourselves to ourselves, which is the textbook function of novel-writing, seems almost beyond the range of anybody in any profession at the moment, but journalists at least enjoy the front-line privilege of being first to announce each new phantasmagoria that heaves in sight and then remains to be explained. They escape the sensation of being left behind which irritates so many novelists, and technically they are excused from the old-fashioned, time-consuming obligation to invent a certain proportion of what they write. Because, like everybody else, they have been educated more in the history of the novel than in journalism, the genre itself sports an illusory newness, which, when the times appear gargantuan—when we feel we need new tools—is a relief.

So it has come to seem ironic that "novel" means new; and there is a clarity to the situation in journalism appropriate to a thriving concern. One notices among the best practitioners a grouping of big-subject men, like David Halberstam and Gay Talese, who trust in legwork and in elbow grease. John McPhee and John Corry look instead to little subjects to enlarge upon, piling up small perfections beautifully. Norman Mailer and Tom Wolfe write in

187

great haste with great gouts of talent, "winging it" like a novelist, not only on the strength of the subject matter but on the strength of their own recklessness. But despite the disarray in fiction enough glory attaches to fighting on regardless, like John Henry, with eclipsed tools, that novelists-turned-journalist sometimes look back to the old problematic, lonely drudgery of novel-writing as movie actors do to the stage: maybe *that* was where the action was.

The recklessness which makes for originality so often grows out of despair that artists between projects will search around for something in their personal lives important to them to smash up, on occasion, just in order to be able to start from scratch. And so the hard times spoken of lately (never mind the necromancer's word "Depression") may give a boost to good writing. Holing up, with less to lose or gain in the way of royalties, his focus once again the recklessness of words and visions, a novelist can take hope as he sees that the role of the novel is no longer primarily to explain, but rather to dramatize, us to ourselves. Here we are, cogs and digits, and on the broader scale, maybe soon to starve or freeze; what better instant to undertake a novel? And journalists—buccaneers and slippery characters ever since their great progenitor Daniel Defoe—flourish anyway in all plague years.

BUT
WHERE
IS HOME?

Who was the appealing
Texan—was it Larry McMurtry?—who went around in a
sweatshirt emblazoned with the legend MINOR REGIONAL
NOVELIST? There is naturally a resentment against New
York City as book capital on the part of writers who have
seated themselves, usually in middle age and after a lot
of peregrinating, in an Athens such as San Francisco,
which they chose in order to escape the crush of competition and to lead the good life, hoping that peace and
comfort and the plaudits of the local Athenians will not
rule out their remaining cosmopolitan. This isn't what is
meant by *regional*, however, and they would be the last
to characterize it so. Regionalism is a prouder banner, a
decent lonely business referring back to Hawthorne in
New England and Twain in Hannibal, to Yoknapatawpha
County, Sauk Center, Sherwood Anderson in Ohio, Hemingway in Michigan. The suspicion exists that most real
writing in America has been regional, and that the re-

markable gifts of such a man as John Dos Passos were perhaps defeated by his not being regional.

But even these eminent authors did not stay in Hannibal and Sauk Center unless they were willing to wait as long for fame as Faulkner did; in our century, at least, they touched base in New York. What they found there must be about the same as what we all find. That is, for instance, in twenty years of writing I have run up against only one publisher who actively went back on his word (and he works out of Boston), but would be hard put now to call up a lifelong fondness for any publisher—the problem with them being that one must always bear in mind that they "say that to all the girls." Our best critic, Alfred Kazin, goes slightly haywire whenever he writes about Jews in the plural, and Wilfrid Sheed, who gives promise of being our next-to-best, is almost equally dotty about the Irish—will claim there is no Irish literary Mafia and imagines himself to have an Antaeus link to the Irish, so that whenever he feels tired or uncertain he reaches out to touch an Irishman. *The New Yorker*, the nation's best magazine, exacts a feudal humility from its contributors—feeds sugar to its pensioners but binds the feet of its young writers to keep them small, rarely permitting them the exhilaration of seeing their work appear. *New York* magazine, by contrast, true to the reputation of New York itself, makes no stir at all to be kind to anybody, old or young, suggesting instead that its writers submit to the central proposition of the magazine itself, which is that more be promised than delivered, a proviso just as

190

limiting to them as to have their feet decoratively bound. But it is inevitable that every magazine have a proviso. Magazines, like newspapers, wind up as a fish's overcoat, if any use is found for them, so that no sooner does one finish deploring the vacuities of a particular issue than it seems cause for wonderment that so much honest cleverness was fitted into it. Furthermore, writers really do not allow themselves to be restricted short of the limits of their gifts. It's no coincidence that *The New Yorker* has published only a minuscule proportion of the work of Bellow, Mailer, Malamud or recent Nabokov, and if one were to look back to the late great era of Faulkner, Hemingway, Thomas Wolfe, Fitzgerald, Steinbeck, Dos Passos, Farrell, Saroyan, one would have to desist from an accounting for very pity. *Esquire,* a lesser magazine, has had a loftier roster, which may just indicate that the best magazines and the best writers stay apart like oil and water. (*New York* magazine hasn't even been able to hold onto its Irishmen.)

Another factor to remember about the relationship between what somebody has called "the oxen and the frogs" is that writers (the oxen) are by no means defenseless. The writers living within the Northeast quadrant who come immediately to mind for excellence are also good at literary politics. Allowing for their differences in beveling, a novelist's trade is, after all, knowing character and plotting, and he can charm with his brusqueness the community of editors and publicists and review specialists if he wants to when he meets them; they should be pushovers.

But, bless him, he may not want to. Or he may choose to write about Texas from Texas, or about Texas, not from either New York or Texas, but from Italy, like William Humphrey. Must he be in the city to push himself and his books? Of course he must. Do some writers of meager talent who live in New York finagle more attention than they deserve? Certainly they do, but not way more, because part of the code of the city is that no matter whom you know, you must be good—people only agree to know you because for the moment they think you're good; that's part of why some writers move to Taos.

So if a writer like Humphrey would have won more fame by living alongside Central Park, are there good writers who live in New York City solely in order to advance themselves? It would be absurd to think so—they live in New York because it activates them—unless perhaps one is thinking about some of the journalists, in whose profession advancing oneself also involves widening one's access to material. Access, for many journalists, is almost everything—that and having the sort of mind that can distinguish, night or day and at an instant's notice, between, say, James Dean and John Dean.

But this business of poking fun at good men is a staple of life in the city. Indeed, many people are in a position to know something about "everybody" because at a late hour in their loneliness they are likely to call some of the same individuals. Writers live in New York City instead of Nebraska for the swarm and rush, and when they age a bit and need to save their energies, they move. If they have gotten rich and successful, though, the folk wisdom which says that originality lives in a garret haunts them and they worry because they moved.

Still, what about the regions; wasn't that where the real writing was? It may well have been, but there's this one problem. There are no regions. There *were* regions, but now there aren't. Houston is rather like Los Angeles, except that, driving in Houston, one finds the thruways posted with signs saying DRIVE FRIENDLY, and for some reason Texans still do. That they do (or tolerate the signs) might interest some novelists, but not many. When I moved to northern Vermont, the real estate agent, himself from "down-country," said as we closed the deal, "I guess in a few years when you finish writing up the stuff you pick up here, you'll go somewhere else and write about that."

Although I blanched a little, having told myself that I was looking for a permanent home, I wondered. The Vermonters all turned out to be old men, however, and by the time I'd talked to them, it didn't seem that I would find the old men of Mississippi any friskier. Though we have a nation, goodness knows, and memories of its regions, we have no regions any more. We have some cities, suburbs, agribusiness, hillbillies, and still the rough outlines of North and South and East and West, but not the regions of regionalism.

And does this mean that writers now must write about marriage and death and fear and joy just as the classic writers did? It does. Luckily, we have been trying to do that all along under the cover of regionalism, and so we can swallow that chunk of the specifications. But where is *home*? Is home going to be only our hats? Can we possibly function like that? Marriage, death and fear and joy under our hats? That's where the question really rests, for architects and pharmacists and you and me.

JOHNNY APPLESEED,
BLUEGRASS,
EGG CREAMS

The saying used to be that
if a boy didn't need to kill his father figuratively in order
to become a man, at least his first step toward manhood
would mean a boot in the old fellow's face. But this is not
quite the case any more, for the simple reason that suicide
has become so prevalent: the suicide of the Nixon kitchen
cabinet, for illustration, which inferentially has taken with
it whole gobs of the nation's rich and influential. Before
that, there was the suicide in Vietnam of an entire generation of mainstream leaders of the Democrats and the
viewpoint that they represented. Recently the custom
has been to speak only of the suicide of the Democratic
party's left, but much more stunning in its effect on the
country had been the catastrophic misjudgment of the
centrist figures, the best of whom, if they are not dead,
are now doing good works at such institutions as the Ford
Foundation or Yale, rather like Profumo doing penance
in his South London slums.

In fact, most of the traditional callings are in trouble—

Wall Street, the unions, soldiering. Even the Pope, as we have been reading for several years, has thought of resigning, and some of the other white-collar professions find themselves in need of an inspector general; hard-pressed reformers are already exerting some weight. Never in living memory in America has the older generation seemed more eager to give up the reins. The whiz kids of the past—I.T.&T.'s Harold Geneen, most prestigious businessman of the sixties, John Mitchell, that decade's best political technician, and General William Westmoreland, going through the ordeal of yet another "honoring" ceremony—perspire and glance out at the world behind the television cameras as if pleading with men younger than they to *take it over, take over the whole damn operation. I'm tired, I'm through!*

It seems unbelievable sometimes, but the most painful eras do pass, power *is* handed on. I look at the people leaving college in their universal blue jeans, and I like the costume: a carpenter's pants, just right for starting from scratch. True, they don't read enough, don't know how to work, don't know how to walk, expect everything to be an "experience," so that experience often eludes them, and are not wholly popular with friends of mine who are college teachers. But they aren't sad like the rest of us. Probably their relaxed eclecticism—the hoboing around and about, the turning from country music to ragtime to Bach—is part of what's going to be needed. America must be reconstructed; we have to rediscover Johnny Appleseed and the Alamo (and like it again), and catfish, bluegrass, egg creams. That is, we've bombed our-

196

selves flat. Liberalism and conservatism are equally in a shambles because of the war, and the people who know straight off what they like about living here are too often the same people who agreed with the bombing. The walruses who have been in charge of the Gross National Product on the home front are being hauled toward the new century, kicking and screaming—toward the idea that the American frontier is at an end and that we cannot continue to "grow" at 10 percent a year, or whatever the current index of business respectability is, but must calm down the "Texan" in us and hold our ground. We must do so—perhaps the people who left college ten years ago can do it—without excising the memory of "Texas," however, gallant panorama that it has been. And this is where the eclecticism of the new young is going to be valuable.

Driving near Houston nowadays, where the real estate business nearly matches the oil industry, one sees, alongside the box turtles and armadillos crushed on the road, a few remaining cowboys hunkered down against the subdivision signpoles. "Crystal Forest," "Roman Forest," "King's Forest," "Forgotten Forest"—the name draws buyers particularly well where there aren't any trees. Around our older big cities, too, everything is changing, because the spirit of any great American metropolis always was salted so heavily with immigration, which is now at an end. City people develop a hard-won impartiality, a malleability that is their best quality, from encountering such an assortment of personalities and pressures, and from snatching their fun where they can.

197

Narcissistic fads like health foods don't do very well in the city. But what is happening is that even sooner than the last dribbles of immigration end, a good many city people are rushing to leave for the suburbs and a blander type of living. The diversity and democracy of small-town life are also being discarded, as farming people move in from farther out. Indeed, except for the fact that more people are traveling abroad, the only increase in eclecticism evidenced lately at all is this peculiar enthusiasm of the young for trying out the styles of the 1950s, the 1930s, the 1890s, or American Indian culture, and feeling at home in any region of the country with a pack on their back.

The way to reconstruct America is to *know* America—which is not exactly a TV spectator sport. Even if we accept for the future a vision of America as a series of concentric suburbs where each family knows only families who are making the same income they do, at least our past, then, must be reevaluated, after the fires of the 1960s in which all of it stood accused of being imperial. And this is what college students have been about, albeit instinctively, since they stopped making history themselves during the demonstrations of that time. Though we may find it disturbing that they don't get as agitated as we do about, say, World War II, it will also be a blessing when our gorges stop rising about Vietnam—when we stop wishing to see an opponent on the issue in handcuffs. The young must do the healing. However they accomplish it—through parody, moviemaking, their penchant for empathizing and communing, or even the regular processes that *we* would use—they must be the ones to reassess our history eventually; there is no one else.

As it happens, once out of childhood, people rarely need to deal with their parents' generation in practical terms. First teachers and then middle management are the buffer, grading them, hiring them, judging what they do. A few years ago this *modus operandi* functioned with considerable clarity, when many of the middle generation went along with the politics of the young activists and seldom made them suffer unduly for what they believed, while at the same time trying to put a brake on the drug scene and taking an in-between view of the sexual revolution, as a rule.

So now top management seeks mainly to resign, to get out of it, asking from the rest of us silence, tolerance and a pension; and middle management will be an ameliorative force as these rediscoveries and reassessments go on. The way should be enviably open for the June graduate to begin remaking the world. With all the water that has gone under the bridge, some fellows simply want to be Marco Polo again, but as many options have opened as have shut down; what has changed is the versatility at hand. Blending and versatility are going to be key words as we try to hang onto our privacy despite our technology —try to hang onto some countryside too. To continue to be both city men and country men, not merely suburban, is to try to grasp past possibilities—and the future would look awfully barren without those ingredients of the past. To a certain extent, if we are to hope for a renaissance, its movers and shakers must be Renaissance men.

We who are middle management right now make quite a deal out of our own versatility. Because it's an effort for us, we're likely to tell everybody that we are planting peach trees at our house in the country, are studying Hebrew, worked years ago on a shrimp boat and are hoping one day to travel to the Hindu Kush. This will all come much more naturally to these young hobos who already at twenty-one may have experimented with being down-and-out in London and Paris, have been in jail here at home on behalf of some lofty cause, and yet have rocked halfway around the world in a groaning airplane after the breakup of a love affair on exotic soil. They do have an extraordinary liquidity—summer vacations, which to an older group sometimes seemed almost too long to fill, now are decidedly too short—and when they go to the movies, it is to see Jeremiah Johnson on the frontier and Andy Warhol's *Heat* on the same bill. Coming into New York City on the bus from New Hampshire, they put on their city shoes, stepping fast, and look left and right, watching ahead on the dark street—man-with-the-bulge-of-a-grocery-sack is all right, man-leading-dog is all right —quick to plunge, to change gaits with this stream of people day or night from which they pick one or another or another to react to.

The city is dying. People don't think of it as a happy place to be any more, which means that the sort of intensity we love it for is beginning to vanish. On 11th Street is a block where sixteen years ago I proposed unsuccessfully to the first girl I loved; it is also the block where one of my wife's closest friends killed herself. On

24th Street I gave an engagement ring to my first wife, on 34th Street I gave one to my second. But in the future these tender or painful moments, concentrating life within such a narrow space, will be spread out to both seacoasts and a half-dozen megalopolises between, with a premium placed on living for the present and traveling light and in planes. Intensity will have to be self-contained; emotion will no longer have any close relation to houses or streets or rivers or fields. Yet precisely because they are different from us, these younger people give promise of being able to manage this change.

Despite the ebbing away of our cities themselves as centers of hubbub and life, nature is giving way to human nature everywhere, so that human nature will soon be the only milieu. Again, though, it seems to me that this generation is on the path to becoming more adept than anybody before at inhabiting a world composed exclusively of human beings, feeling in its element there, slipping through a hundred encounters a day, not-meeting-the-eye or meeting-the-eye as the case may be, and apprehending quickly everything from agonistic behavior, as a zoologist would call it, to love, guile, good cheer and fear. Of course, if we are to do away with nature and with the animal kingdom and psychically survive, the first necessity is that we retain the animality of man. Indeed, one could claim that the last stronghold of the animal world will be in the sex life of man, and that, since the actual baby-germinating purpose of sex has become a shadow of what it once was, part of the reason we are about the most sexual of mammals is not only our present insistence on pleasure for pleasure's sake at all times, but a deep, constructive and subconscious grasping for an immediate bodily existence, now that those wonderfully totemic and comradely creatures whom we have depended upon for so long are gone from our lives.

In the act of sex we hook up with so much of importance, a whole spontaneous level of life which otherwise is being destroyed. Although the best naturalist writers, like Konrad Lorenz, can still write about an afternoon's animal-like basking or roam in the woods as a respite from their "higher" lives, at this point most of us aren't capable of much more than enjoying reading about it. We'd be unable to lie still like a crocodile on a mudbank of the Danube for four hours, in "animal nirvana," as Lorenz can. But during sex we dig down into our ancestry for a while, thrashing, loping, wetting ourselves, kicking, pulsing, losing track of time, feeding atavistically in mollusk beds way back below time. It is the one form of rapture left to many of us, and though it's encouraging that some of the young hobos I'm discussing care more about wild things and wild places than their fathers did, even if it has become too late now for these to be saved, it's also encouraging that they are better at sex as well.

They're better at sex because they feel natural with it, but, presumably in conjunction with the other experimenting that they are doing, at the moment they are more engaged in studying the samenesses of the two sexes than the differences. This might seem contradictory, unless it can be interpreted as a more thorough exploration of the sex drive, combining rather than separating all the strands. There is another contradiction, however—a huge, happy, pregnant, lopsided one. We see this slippery, versatile, sophisticated generation swiftly advancing into a fantastically complicated, well-lubricated new universe of opportunities; yet all around are innumerable cookie-cut, ticky-tacky suburbs which the architects are preparing for them to live in, and a systems-analysis set-up is being invented to regiment their lives to what we are told will be an unparalleled degree. Their limberness, education, overexperience, the travel bug that possesses them, their social and sexual daring, the new habit of self-indulgence, along with the decline of marriage and even of friendship as institutions, all argue against the kind of dreary conventionality that regularly is predicted as their lot.

When I was in college one of my friends was a man of sixty, a Wall Street law partner of John Foster Dulles and other bigwigs. What I especially remember him remarking about was how "frightening" it sometimes felt to belong to the generation in power, whose members were the recognized authorities, not simply in government, but in any given business or field: to realize, as each of them did, how little they really knew, how much must always be improvised, how often they just shut their eyes and hoped. As I get into my forties I begin seeing firsthand what he meant. In a modest way, acquaintances of mine have become authorities; I too have areas of expertise. Yet we know next to nothing. If we are lucky, we may know somebody to call who knows a bit more. Since this is always going to be true—God save us, anyway, from the perfect expert—what intrigues me about these young graduates is not their potential for expertise, but their versatility. If they keep on growing more and more versatile than we ever were, their world may be better than ours.

VIRGINIE
AND THE
SLAVES

In New York City a white man meeting four blacks on the street may quaver if he's alone, but the next day, flying to the Deep South, he sees fear on the faces of a group of Negroes on a country road when he stops for directions. They call him "Cap'm" and go right into the goofy set of mannerisms of song and story. The pretty girl among them has kinked her hair tightly into the waffle-iron pattern that slaves used to present to Massa at the commissary every Sunday before they got their pickled pork and kernel corn to last them through the week.

Traveling is not the undertaking that it used to be, when one progressed through every climatic, topographic change that finally culminated in the warm air or fine scenery we were in search of. By ship and train and jalopy we traveled as far vertically, just jouncing up and down. But now we jet abruptly into a softer climate, not ready for the balminess, which may seem unearned, or perhaps earned only professionally, like a stiff drink in the evening. And so in order not to feel like samplers, most of us manage to substitute for the old, flavorful, laborious transitions a kind of simultaneity of awareness: of what the Mississippi smells like at New Orleans and the face of the Rockies at Rifle, Colorado. When you go worldwide with this, meandering in Place St. Sulpice and thinking about where you'll be staying in Izmir tomorrow night, it creates an opportunity for either a catastrophe or a triumph of equilibrium.

To mention the Old South brings to mind plantation houses, just as "New England" calls up white steeples and green maples. But the South was quintessentially rural, and before the Civil War was more a matter of flatboats freighting bales of cotton on the rivers and canal excavations in the swamps than palace architecture. New England, too, was primarily a world center for sheep ranching rather than in the maple business; the occasional Greek Revival house, with portico and fading pillars, was probably constructed with money from Merino wool at the same time as the South's cotton mansions. In the South there is a certain sisterly spirit toward New Englanders, so that when I've roamed about with Vermont license plates in the guise of a Yankee, although I've gotten gimpy glances from the carloads of whites who fought the civil-rights fights of the 1960s, the older ladies of the upper-middle class were quite prepared to welcome me. Even today the War for Southern Independence, as they call it, preoccupies them, and any traditional foe of the Confederacy is to be embraced before the barbarians from

Los Angeles and Phoenix who swoop through en route to Florida.

It is such older ladies who have bought and restored the mansions that remain along the lower Mississippi—a frighteningly accidental process. The Mississippi itself wiped out a good many houses that survived the Civil War, especially along the wet lowlands of the west bank and on the east bank below Baton Rouge where sugar cane was grown. Others were demolished when the high levees were built, or else have just lately fallen victim to the veritable Ruhr of industry—Exxon, American Cyanamid and Union Carbide—which has usurped so much of the east bank. One sees cows on the levee, and cattle egrets that stalk along beside their feet to catch the grasshoppers that leap. Down next to the water are patches of willow and cottonwood, and sometimes bootleg little gardens with scarecrows with pie pans swinging from their fists, and the old "borrow pits," where the levee dirt was dug and where the fishing always was the best. Nevertheless, below Baton Rouge the bridges of the tankers and the crane booms of the freighters loom taller than the levee. There is the smell and steam of industry, jointed and shiny like a row of erector sets, and endless lines of tank cars waiting to be filled. This is the New South, which can be romanticized as foolishly as was the Old.

Throughout a tatty century these isolated, vainglorious houses were stoned and partied in by vandals, dismembered by treasure hunters; probably more of them were set afire by fraternity boys than by Abe Lincoln's soldiers.

One looks for them between slag heaps and sulphur piles, and finds an upstairs now restored but the ground floor still scarred by campfires, the caretaker a stumbling, toothless white man who lives with his chickens in a shack in the yard. At "Ashland-Belle Helene" (twenty-eight white columns), which has for neighbors Shell, Texaco and Allied and Borden Chemical, cattle were sheltering inside until only twenty years ago, when Clark Gable and Clint Eastwood came to make films.

Such houses are in a fix that might temper the wrath of an old-time abolitionist, since their history concerns him too. Sometimes the sole trace left (and always the first sight one comes upon) is the splendid live oaks, boled like elephants and lavish in the reach of their limbs. But because the State of Louisiana has done nothing to assist in their protection—other than buying a house in West Feliciana Parish where John James Audubon lived during the summer of 1821 and another associated with the Longfellow-Evangeline State Park—they have become the hobby-horse of individual ladies. In the course of touring a string of them, one hears about each new owner's Christmas customs, each new family's summer home. Alongside the Napoleon sofas, walnut armoires and Italian altarpieces will be the son's silver costume from Mardi Gras, when he was Crown Prince of his dad's krewe, and Son himself in a kitsch portrait over the mantel of Carrara marble.

General Nathaniel Banks, who did most of the Union's fighting in these parts, has not the reputation of a Sherman, except that in 1864, in retreat through the Natchitoches district of northwest Louisiana after the defeat of his Red River campaign, he did some gratuitous burning. A party of hungry skirmishers would carry along a bucket of tar to brush against the walls of a house where they thought food should be obtainable, and if the residents didn't ante up they'd strike a match. There were two types of grand household: that from which the women had already fled in fear of the Union troops and their own servants, and that in which they stood their ground and saw their possessions fare well, on the whole. At "Parlange" the mistress feted General Banks at a fancy banquet and had her slaves barbecue a beef for the enlisted men under the looping oaks out on the lawn, so that she didn't have to stash her silverware in the stock pond. But slaves, envious neighbors or white jayhawkers might loot or start a fire too, and as a Northern trooper named Lawrence Van Alstyne wrote in his diary across the Mississippi from "Parlange," the sight of the scarred bodies of the field hands "beat all the anti-slavery sermons ever yet preached." This neighborhood was about as far down the river as anybody could be sold.

Vermonters have a saying when they hate someone: "I'd like to get him in my hog pen!" That regimen of slops and mud, and finally to be strung up by the heels and feel his throat cut. That there were few slaves in New England was fortunate both for the slaves and for New England, and certainly there is enough brutality in the famous parsimony of New Englanders to match up comparably with the bullying air of the young oil nabobs of the Gulf Coast. Still, since hogs are only hogs, and parsimony, hiding itself, continually dies back, as a practical matter nothing in the ordinary experience of a Yankee, I discovered, is going to prepare him for the extremes, as lush as nature's, of opulence alongside privation—the violent corrugations—of life in Louisiana.

Once the jungle had been pruned back, what this lower Mississippi region provided was topsoil from the nation's entire midsection, pilfered alluvially, along with sixty inches of rainfall a year and a 320-day growing season. But these benefits came accompanied at first by wolves and bears and panthers, 15-foot alligators, and fevers that killed more slaves than harsh treatment and more masters than feuding. The cypresses alone were so intimidating that a German immigrant who had for weeks been clearing a bit of bank near the big river turned into the wrong bayou one morning, and every bend seemed perfectly familiar, every tupelo gum tree and cypress overhanging his canoe, lugubriously festooned with weeping moss, seemed like a specific adversary he thought he had laid low—until he recognized that the vindictive forest must have re-created itself overnight to stand just as it had before, and he gave up and paddled hard for New Orleans.

A man was known for his hound dogs—such a breed as the Catahoula cur or "leopard dog," which made the woods less formidable and routed out the hogs for butchering in the fall. After a plague of caterpillars in 1793, indigo faded as a crop (it was also rumored to have affected the health of the slaves). Then the wetlands were planted with sugar cane, usually by Creole settlers from New Orleans, a method for granulation having been invented at about this time. The hillier, drier country went into cotton. Being further from the river and the French city, it was occupied a little later, often by Americans of English ancestry who had journeyed across the Appalachians from the eastern states after the U.S. purchase of Louisiana in 1803. Rice needed such a thorough, constant wetting that it grew best along the stable bayous of southwest Louisiana—Bayou Teche, Vermilion River and other Cajun strongholds. Therefore the cotton mansions naturally tended to resemble the great houses of Virginia, while those built with sugar or rice money might wear a French patina. The older French ones are influenced by Spanish architecture as well, especially with the feature of an outside staircase, because under Louisiana's period of Spanish administration (1764–1800) a house was taxed as a single-story dwelling as long as it did not boast a stairwell indoors.

The Spanish governors ruled rather benignly, considering that most of the citizenry were French. They even welcomed more Frenchmen from Europe and Canada, the "Cajuns" being Acadian refugees pushed out of Nova Scotia during and following the French and Indian Wars. City Creole and country Cajun kept apart, and do so still. Besides them and the Spanish and Canary Islanders, the German settlers, the high-class, black-earth French, the high-class, black-earth English-Americans, the red-dirt, dirt-poor American backwoodsmen, and all the slaves, there was a substantial contingent of Irishmen, who bestowed upon downtown New Orleans its Brooklyn accent ("foist," "hoid," "boid"). No other Southern state remains

211

such a crosshatch of bailiwicks, with blacks so black, French so French, rich so rich, and rednecks so redbone: a gastronomic, tacky city, surrounded by hardshell, diehard hillbillies.

The different mansion tours are modestly priced and usually improvised. At the steamboat-gothic edifice known as "San Francisco" (not after the city but from the expression *mon saint-frusquin,* "my last red cent"—and indeed the young fellow who built it died soon afterwards), the lady in residence has "trained," as they say in the trade, two black servants to speak certain key phrases and herself sits downstairs to answer further inquiries. At "Asphodel," on the other hand, the lady of the manor says her piece into a tape recorder which the maid carries from room to room, plugging and unplugging it as you progress, meanwhile dusting and sweeping continually. "Madewood," on Bayou Lafourche, is another house whose original owner, a Colonel Pugh—altogether his family owned eighteen plantations and three thousand slaves by the time of the Civil War—died of fret and yellow fever before he could enjoy the premises. The present cook, however, leaves her kitchen, wry and brisk, to show a visitor around. "Corinthian columns inside, Ionic columns outside in front, Doric columns outside in back." At "Evergreen," near Edgard, Louisiana, even the brick privies were built like Greek temples. And the tour of "Houmas House" is led by a crisp young black woman. "Made by the slaves," she says, pointing at a pewter chandelier, her tone as noncommittal as two saucers clinking.

A bit of crewelwork at "Houmas House" gives the

slogan of the day: "Yours is the Earth and everything in it." One sees a butterfly-pegged floor, a canopied bed of tiger maple, a kneehole desk, a secretary carved out of crotch mahogany. The wall ovens were fired the day before a banquet and then the fire removed for baking. The young white "gemmelmen" roosted on their own in twin white *garconnières*, which they could spray with tomcat squirt at night, as rank as goats, and the ladies in the main house needn't know.

"Rosedown," in the former cotton center of St. Francisville, is another product of the copious thirty years or so preceding the Civil War. With its Versailles garden and eleven fireplaces in its sixteen rooms, it has been restored with Texas oil money and is in the custody of a squadron of retired schoolteachers who seem to have geared themselves to appear redoubtable enough to make the $4 fee worthwhile. The tour is roped and formal, and they exaggerate their accents for toniness more even than for geography. There are Aubusson carpets, a swan-shaped cradle, a Chippendale birdcage, Mallard and Belter furniture, smoke bells over the many oil lamps, a punkah, and pull ropes in most of the rooms that lead to bells of varying tones by which the servants could figure out where they were required to go. One prize bed, intended for Henry Clay, has bedposts nearly fourteen feet high; another is a sort of miniature fashioned from papier-mâché inlaid with mother-of-pearl. The prettiest room is the breakfast room, with a collection of green lacquer furniture and a wood chandelier. The six columns in front of the front door are cypress trunks; the walls and floors are cypress. There are summer houses in the garden and a dovecote beside the pond, an outdoor furnace for boiling soap and scalding pigs, and an enormous kitchen shed. The ensemble was built to go with thirty-five hundred acres and four hundred and fifty slaves, and not till 1955 did the family finally "daughter out."

One can stay close by at "Asphodel" in a slave cabin, of all places, air-conditioned, where the food is good. "The Cottage" is the other fancy inn in the vicinity of St. Francisville. Built of cypress from an inner Spanish structure which dates to 1795, it has the loveliest possible setting and smells of jasmine and honeysuckle in the month of May. The floors are going cattywomp, the wallpaper is original; one sleeps in a hip-high, silken-canopied, 1810 fourposter bed, and a bandannaed black serves breakfast. The principal past owner was Thomas Butler, who owned twelve plantations across the Mississippi and was a member of Congress. Many of his outbuildings have been preserved—his law office, milk house, smokehouse, carriage house, commissary, and three of twenty-five slave hovels, each of which had two rooms and housed two families.

"Oakley," the state-owned house memorializing Audubon's stay in Louisiana, was also begun around 1800. It was built for a plantation of twenty-nine hundred acres and a hundred and thirty-five slaves; outside, under loblolly pines, the cotton rows are still discernible. The Colonial Dames and D.A.R. have furnished it comfortably with Federal Period appurtenances, so that of all the restored manor houses it is probably the most natural. On the walls are Audubon's chipping sparrow, tufted duck, red-cockaded woodpecker and cerulean warbler, and there are leather fire buckets, pewter plates (called "poor man's silver"), a spinning-weaving room and an inventory of slaves, in which I noticed that a man in his forties like me was still considered to be worth the top price of seven hundred dollars, as were others ten years younger or even just nineteen.

Herefords and anguses graze in the fields around town nowadays, because after the boll weevil's inroads in the 1930s, cotton never did come back; the terrain defeated the modern machinery that made cotton so profitable again in Mississippi's flat delta counties north of Vicksburg. A lot of pine was planted instead, Crown Zellerbach has erected a paper mill and there's a sweet-potato canning factory and a concrete-mat casting plant of the U.S. Army Corps of Engineers at riverside. But all of this scarcely dents the unemployment in this old plantation region, with more black people than white and much miserable poverty. Even the panel trucks that sell snap beans and tomatoes along Highway 61 bear a scrawl on cardboard: "We accept food stamps." Vee's squatty 5¢–10¢ store and the Boll Weevil Cafe with its planked porch are something of a link to slavery if one reads people's faces aright—screwed tight, as if they had been baked in a crucible. And when a white man around here speaks of the slaves or the slaves' life, a sneaky smile captures his mouth, as though he were remembering a rich practical joke.

Sometimes I found my mind didn't take the tour as planned. I'd look into the hostess's face—or another visitor's—to see what kind of mistress she would have made, and it was never encouraging. Inside the house, with a forbiddingly unreconstructed matron speaking of the six hundred thousand homemade bricks under one's feet—a platform eight feet high, before they'd even started with the cypress and the *bousillage* plastering—all the while pulling the bell ropes and pointing to a punkah fan and to a water jar suspended from a hook in the ceiling, to be pulled a thousand times and cooled, I would panic slightly; I wanted to be *out*, as though some sudden reversion could cause these tasks to be delegated to me. But then outside, beyond the Spanish dagger and the century plants, the redbud and crape myrtle trees, I'd walk around the immense house at a distance of a hundred yards, wanting painfully to get *in*. On the one side, the sweating discipline of men, and on the other, the impossible discipline of women, while in a wider circle all around had been the jungle, with cottonmouths, six-foot rattlers and biting bugs. Even the runaways who learned to live in it and fish and snare, putting the wateriest parts between them and the master's hounds, seem to have been drawn back, not only in order to resupply themselves, but for another look at that blinding, concise, white house.

Of them all, "San Francisco" alarmed me most, because of its pop-Gothic gingerbread and rococo scrollwork, the fluted pillars' decorative iron devices on its double galleries, the snake-eyed narrow windows high up. I gazed at it from atop the Mississippi's levee, and walked around and around. It had a blaring quality, a fearful and tyrannical sense—even the looming twin cisterns built of

cypress wood and holding eight thousand gallons apiece
—because I couldn't possibly imagine myself as the master
at such a place, only as a slave, and whatever mind had
lived there as its master had been a tinkerer's, a monkey's.

The headquarters of the East Louisiana State Hospital
for mental illness, at Jackson, is an imposing white plantation mansion, and so is the administrative building of the
U.S. National Leprosarium at Carville, on the Mississippi,
the only leper colony in the United States. Angola State
Prison, at Tunica, which is close to St. Francisville, is another location to visit for a whiff of the old woefulness
which accompanied this splendor; there you can still see
Negroes crouch and scurry. The steamboat captains, with
that waterman's relish for the high and low tidemarks of
life, used to salute the lepers with three bawdy toots when
they slid by, and no doubt did the same at Tunica when
passing a convict gang. The river itself was so unpredict-
able, so rife with contradictions, that the savageries of
slavery must have seemed less weird right alongside.
And yet the best place for a runaway to head for is
said to have been the woodyards on both banks, where a
freemasonry of axmen and raftsmen existed and where
he might manage to hole up successfully if he could hold
his own.

From the army, some of us remember the sergeant's
familiar warning, derived from slavery and hollered in the
drizzly dawn: "I'll have your *ass*. Your souls may still belong to God but your ass is mine!" In fact of course it
wasn't, but the most remarkable omission in American
literature is the virtual absence of this unnerving and dra-

matic subject, going so against the country's grain. Melville and Hawthorne, Thoreau, Whitman, Emerson and even Twain touched upon it only briefly, never finding it obsessive, compared to the nineteenth-century Russian masters, their contemporaries. Presumably serfdom seemed so much in character with the Russian national spirit to Turgenev, Chekhov, Gogol, Tolstoy, that to try to excise their continual pain and preoccupation with the question would be to rifle out the heart of much of their best work. By contrast, our Northerners could regard slavery as the plague of another region if they chose to, and something of an abstraction besides, because the slaves were Africans and black. More recently Willa Cather, Robert Penn Warren and William Styron, writers with Southern roots, have tried to come to grips with the matter, but not convincingly. Faulkner, who with his marvelous imaginative grasp was the obvious candidate, seems to have flinched from depicting the reality of slavery, preferring to deal with it as a subsequent "stain," or, in his best brush with the idea, by means of another device of removal—the master being the comic obese Indian chief, Moketubbe, in the Indian story, "Red Leaves." Thus, instead of a literature to set next to the Russian masterpieces which record the tragedy of slavery, we have *Uncle Tom's Cabin* and *Gone With the Wind*.

Slaves who lived within the unit of a middle-class white family had a more interesting time of it, for better or worse, than in the regimented hoeing gangs, although the Big House gradually became the very symbol of slavery (and later prison parlance). A great house was cooler during the summer than an ordinary dwelling, and provided ways to employ a surplus labor force (those bricks!); also to consume slathers of money that otherwise might not have been so easily spent. Beyond that, it represented luxury and power and monumentalized the ego of a man and wife who lived like petty gods, a centerpiece to focus every eye on what the labor of the plantation was all about. The slave quarters were seldom far away, which indicates a continuing wish on the part of the white folk for intimacy with their darkies. "Belle Grove," a 75-room manor on the Mississippi constructed with sugar money, had dungeons with barred windows in the very basement. At "Magnolia Plantation House" in Derry, Louisiana, the stocks for those who were unruly still stand underneath the veranda. At "Oakland," on the Cane River, in the cellar under the master's bedroom was a little room with a trap door for the girl who was kept there to respond to his summons at night. And in the formal gardens at "The Shadows," on Bayou Teche, bordered now with hand-shaped bricks from the slave cottages, is a sundial on which is engraved the grim homily: "Abundance is the daughter of economy and work." David Weeks, who built the house, stood seven feet tall and must have been a frightening sight. He got hold of ten thousand acres of the most fecund sugar land in North America, which since his death has been found to overlie Louisiana's fattest salt deposits, if there is a lesson in that.

Many slaves, arriving in New Orleans as *Africains bruts*, originated in Senegal. (And some of the local doctors made their fortunes buying and speculating on those who'd sickened on the trip.) After 1808, when this import trade was banned in the United States, Negroes were brought in coffles overland from Virginia and the Carolinas to Tennessee and down the river, as the old tobacco fields gave out and eastern slaves themselves turned into a cash crop. Men and women who were removed to the cane country by their own masters were aghast at the bodeful change in countenance that came over these individuals where so much money could be made. Wearing a breechcloth in the summer, in winter a wool hooded monk's cape, they were worked from before sunup to dark, except in the fall, the cane-grinding season, when the sugar mills ran around the clock. Indeed, one can still see a cane-rich lady's mouth bulge full-of-nails when she speaks of that tough spell of the year. The cotton planter's reckoning with his slaves during the picking season came at the weighing scales, if he hadn't ridden herd on them rigorously enough all day in the field. And from boyhood on, it must be borne in mind, managing slaves encompassed all the macho importance of a cowboy out West cutting horses, or what is now entailed in driving a car well. For a severe beating, the person was staked to the ground in a St. Andrew's cross and whipped from the heels to the neck, a hole being dug in the ground in order to accommodate the stomach in cases of pregnancy.

"What is more remarkable is that the Creole women are often much crueler than the men," wrote C.C. Robin, a French diarist, in his *Voyage to Louisiana* (1807). "Their slow and soft demeanor, the meticulous tasks which they impose, are given in a manner of apathetic indolence, but if a slave does not obey promptly enough, if he is slow to interpret their gestures or their looks, in an instant they are armed with a formidable whip. No longer is this the arm which can hardly support a parasol. . . . Once she has ordered the punishment of one of these unfortunate slaves, she watches with a dry eye . . . she counts the blows and if the arm of him who strikes begins to falter or if the blood does not run fast enough, she raises her voice in menacing tones. . . . They require to see this horrible spectacle repeated at intervals. In order to revive themselves, they require to hear the sharp cries and to see again the flow of blood."*

At several houses you can inspect the bronze bell which ruled the hours, as soft and greeny-looking as a melon now, but there is nothing else from that era, except the fruits of the women's shopping expeditions to Paris. No whips that paid the bills, no handcuffs, no belled iron collars, no wooden "goggles," which weighed three pounds and were attached to bands of iron around a runaway's ankles—a kind of caricature of Mercury's wings—to lash him if he trotted, and no immersion stool. "Tried the cold water on her Ladyship," wrote Bennet H. Barrow, a rather temperate fellow, a resident of St. Francisville, in his journal, after a whipping had not worked on a slave girl. With all the nostalgic exhibits of kitchen utensils, farming equipment, the dainty bibelots, the encyclopedia of gra-

* Robin, *Voyage to Louisiana*, translated by Stuart O. Landry Jr. (New Orleans: Pelican Publishing Co., 1966), pp. 239–40.

cious furnishings, I saw not a single whip preserved at the mansions I visited, though the state museum at "Oakley" did have a slave trap (unlabeled) outside—like a bear trap but without teeth so that the man's leg would not be pulverized.

In a cement-block restaurant on the highway, drinking Dixie Beer with rib-eye steak and smothered okra, I listened to several cattle dealers tell about the nigger who got treed inside a cattle truck when they had let a bull in when he wasn't looking—how he scrambled up the walls and along the ceiling, clinging like a monkey as it hooked at him, the whole crowd laughing till he saved himself. It wasn't that they had wanted him killed—he was popular enough—they had wanted him *all but* killed, reduced to a parody of any man's nightmare. Another fellow, a trapper, told how a nigger last winter waved his truck down and begged for the carcass of a coon he'd skinned. "Man, I just threw three coons away!" he'd yelled.

With the exception of those doughty Brooklyn Irishmen in New Orleans, the coastal and delta South still speaks with the drawl the African slaves fell into as they stepped off the boat and began to rassle with the king's English. And since Southerners remain charmed by their own speech patterns (as, admittedly, most of the rest of us are charmed) slavery can be credited for that. It also bestowed upon them two centuries' worth of scapegoats to burlesque every other man's worst night sweats and dreads: of losing children, wife and home, of hunger, cold, and being whopped and bestialized. Having before them a black populace who were actually undergoing, in a

horrific kind of shadow show, events that are usually confined to one's bad dreams, Southerners as a group perhaps
tended to become less introspective than Northerners.
They were, in a sense, *released*; yet at the same time they
were also mesmerized by the fact that they lived with the
dream made real. Their "tragic view" has taken the form
of an abstractedness, the absent-mindedness which is
peculiar to many Southerners and has been reinforced by
the feeling, widely spread, that whatever the task, if somebody will just wait a little, other hands and other backs
will get it done. Always, however, they reserved one prov-
ince—violence—to themselves, which is why they still fly
off the handle so extravagantly when crossed and why
they fight for their country and love football.

But hot under the collar and abstracted as they got, it
was great fun being an old-school Southerner. This is
evident to me whenever I go poking around with a white-
haired gent I know, quail-hunting, netting half a pail of
crawfish, and gossiping with the different landowners
whose fences we must climb. Then after dark we go fishing
on the bayou with a Coleman lantern dragged behind the
boat on a raft made from a tire which draws thousands of
bugs and slews of little fish and some fine big ones. He
has his pal from New Orleans along, a white-blonde in her
late forties with shrewd eyes and an aggravated mouth—
a V-shaped, stripper's face—who's fat in all the right and
all the wrong places, and splits her evenings and weekends
between my friend and another aging tiger. She's a beau-
tician, a soldierly and slangy woman whose freedom and
friendship with men is her strength here in the back coun-

try, where the woodsy women seem either rather mousy or have the same jumpy appeal as deer. A Yankee like me she teases about putting the niggers "in a vat," and with her fantasy of riding in a carriage pulled by twelve chained bucks, and her with a horsewhip—nonetheless, it really *is* her fantasy. She says New Orleans is "careforgotten. We don't care who you are or what you have or where you come from if you know how to have a good time." She grew up in Biloxi, on the Mississippi Gulf Coast, feeling with her bare toes for soft-shell crabs hiding in the salt grass at night for Sunday dinner. She says her mother was Italian but at fourteen she "crossed the line" and captured a twenty-one-year-old Protestant of the old stock. In this town, she says, she would have left, by golly, at the age of five.

In the motel parking lot, when we pass another white-haired gentleman escorting a bleached blonde, my friend and he exchange meaningful nods. "Well, how are you? Good to see you. How you holdin' up?"

The other thing that my friend likes to do when visiting his boyhood stamping grounds is to chat with the "nigras," especially those who are his contemporaries. It's a man's business, fiddling and dickering with the nigras, and it is simply untrue to claim, as political liberals often do, that only the Negro in the parley realizes that the bonhomie is a charade. The grin my friend wears is ripe with import and his eyes shine, asking the "boy" where his boss is—a grin for back-of-the-barn—while the "boy," scattering yessuhs, goes into a kind of stationary buck and wing. It's semisexual, not much different from when my gent is chaffing a "brown-meat-and-brown-gravy" whore, and even when there is no nigger around and he's just telling nigger stories, his smile is like that of a boy who's fingering his genitalia. Like frogging, fishing, shooting rabbits, masturbating, it is good country fun to hang about with the niggers—more a man's proper activity than a woman's, and more of a boy's than a grown man's. Niggers, or at least the fun of niggers, go so much with boyhood that this may be part of the reason why they are called "boy." And though most of the menace in the tone has waned and everybody knows nigger servitude is ending, men my friend's age know that just as it is surely going to end, it won't end so soon that they will have to do without it in their own lifetimes; they can relax in that regard. Besides the ripe, erotic grin, the other expression they wear when on the subject is vaguely secretive, like that which goes with talk of money corruption up North—that of a man who has "a good thing going."

As for the violence, recollections of Negroes tipped into the water and run down with a motorboat or beaten to death with an oar for crabbing in the wrong bayou (the offense also invariably boyish), one must eavesdrop on the poorer white men—top shirt button buttoned—or a man who began life poor and still sees no necessity to keep quiet about such incidents. "Oooo-*oooo*," he'll say, recalling with a small smile those ole boys who'd got so *mad*.

To relive the relationship between owner and slave we can consider how we treat our cars and dogs—a dog exercising a somewhat similar leverage on our mercies and a good automobile being comparable in value to a slave in those days. We can look in the big cities for the casualties or drive the back roads of the Black Belt where the stay-putters remain. Historically, there has been incredible procrastination on the matter, beginning with the negligence of Washington and Jefferson, who disapproved of slavery but made no provision for moderating it in the manipulative late 1780s before regional patterns rigidified. Because remorse has never been America's strong suit, Reconstruction had hardly got started before forced labor was reinstituted and, at least in the form of convict-leasing, grew so bad that in Louisiana the mortality rate reached 14 percent in 1881. Eventually there must be some provision for the other reality: the fact that these plantations were also archipelagos of suffering. There must be a "Black's Plantation" museum too.

As it is, "Catalpa," in St. Francisville, and "Parlange," which is across the Mississippi on an oxbow called False River, are occupied by descendants of the ante-bellum tenants, so that while listening to these old women painstakingly display their wares, one can catch a glimpse, even through the obfuscation of family folklore, of the strange feral existence led here before and just after the Civil War.

At "Catalpa," Mamie Ford Thompson shows Audubon's portrait of her beautiful great-grandmother (for whose safety's sake he was purportedly dismissed from his post as her tutor); then another of her grandmother, who she says collected a hundred proposals. She herself is a modest, hospitable woman in a drab blue sack of a suit, and serves sherry to visitors, saying twelve of America's first

226

nineteen millionaires lived here along the lower river. There's a Sèvres whale-oil lamp to prove it, an ingenious whale-oil coffeemaker, Meissen and Venetian vases, a ladies' cuspidor, rose-petal jars for scent, low chairs for small-boned people, numerous silver services that were buried in burlap during the War, and the curved silver crumber used at "Rosedown" during the seven-course dinners when she dined there with her relatives before the family turned land-poor. The pride of "Catalpa" is the elliptical, quarter-mile drive lined with live oaks planted as acorns in 1814, with conch shells under them, pink inside, most of which the tourists have stolen but which the slaves used to wash regularly in the bass pond. Azaleas bloom pink in May and hydrangeas and magnolias in June, set off by the hanging moss.

Mrs. Parlange, across the river, is a tiny innocent, showing silk-and-mahogany bookcases, swords, tea boxes, applewood beds from Paris, a Boulle cabinet, candle vases that served the dual purpose of giving light and of keeping the night teakettle hot, a bubble-maker for enlivening drinks, an ebony table inlaid with gold and tortoise shell. It's a dear tour, comprising the usual mix of gewgaws and museum pieces, good portraits and atrocious ones—e.g., a belle forced into marriage who died of a heart attack on her wedding night and was buried in her white dress. The house was built more than two hundred years ago of mud-and-deer-fur *bousillage* framed with cypress posts on a cool raised brick base, with dovecotes set in front and a Southern garden of mimosas and camellias (as well as chameleons). Mrs. Parlange speaks in New Orleans Brook-

lynese of ice brought down the Mississippi during her girl-
hood for summer champagne balls, and about how no
Creole whose origins cannot be traced back to the eight-
eenth century is clean of nigger blood. Her own mama
married a New York Dutch Yankee, because at the balls in
New Orleans that season he changed his white gloves before each dance and spoke French with the accent of
France.

Across False River, however, is what Mrs. Parlange
calls "the chickencoop," where the *coureurs de bois*
settled. These "runners of the woods"—French trappers
and woodsmen who rafted down from the Great Lakes
region instead of coming by sea through New Orleans—
have slivered the shoreline into splintery freeholdings, as
along the St. Lawrence, through their practice of dividing
land into equal parcels for the next generation. By contrast, the Parlanges struggled to save at least two thousand of their acres intact. One young man married the
mortgage holder's daughter, and Virginie Parlange, a
stylish *maman*, after having entertained both General
Banks and then General Dick Taylor of the Confederacy
in 1864, called together her slaves under an oak tree and
told them Abe Lincoln had freed them but that she would
hock her silver in New Orleans to feed them if they would
stay and work. This latest Mrs. Parlange's confused *pied
noir* face so guilelessly recaptures that instant as she talks
—a wildness, a pity, a misery which otherwise would be
irretrievable—that somehow it is possible to stand in the
shoes not only of Virginie but of one of the two hundred
slaves: damned if they accepted, damned if they did not.

The South in the years immediately following the War dug down into its stock of rural savvy, scraping by on possum meat and poke salad, but later was to show off those white pillars as substantiation of the claim that this, like other slave societies, had been a golden age. The slave who dwells in me found it impossible to be inside the houses, yet impossible to be altogether outside, because it *was* a golden age for somebody, all right; there were happy people here. Apologists gloss over the wretchedness of the institution by pointing to the millhands of Massachusetts and to the European navvies who labored through these swamps, building roads and railroads where yellow fever was too pervasive to risk the health of a slave. But of course the well-turned-out visitors who drive up to "Rosedown" on their way to Florida are descendants not of the slaves but of the navvies and millhands. Sometimes, for a quarter of an hour, one feels in the position of the young gemmelman of the house, to whom every nearby creature belonged; sometimes like a traveler lodged in the "stranger's room" opening only onto the veranda (these levee grandees were so free with their hospitality that they couldn't always let the guest inside the house); and sometimes in the winter clodhoppers of a field hand glimpsing the hipped roof while marching to chop cane.

Sugar cane is sweetest if harvested after a cold snap—just as maple sap is best when a night frost has brought up the sugar content—and so the hardest work on a sugar plantation coincided with the end of the fall. Some of the landowners even concocted a ceremony to wind it up. The biggest cane-cutter would be set dancing around the final stalk, which was tasseled with a bit of ribbon, in what the overseers conceived as resembling a tribal "dance." Then he cut the cane and carried it, with all the prime hands behind him, to Marse's house. Marse would come out on the white gallery with the mistress and Mizz Judith and Marse Alexander and raise a glass of wine to the good harvest in front of the hands, and let them each enjoy a cup of rum. Then they gave their massa a cheer and he had their Chrismus gifs distributed, which were the tow shirts, capes, pants and shoes they would wear while plowing, planting, hoeing, chopping and cooking down the sugar crop next year.

Once in Jefferson County, Texas, across the Sabine River from Louisiana, I stumbled on a ranch of umpteen hundred acres which struck a note of terror in me. I'd come there wolfing, and since there were few wolves, I'd had plenty of chance to see a more embracing predation. To catch a horse the cowmen mesmerized him with their arms extended, snake-to-bird, and when they waved their magic arms at a big bull, riding in irresistible circles around him, the animal soon folded.

Wolfing about the bends and elbows of the country, one has plenty of opportunities for recapitulating history. For blundering upon an alligator hunter with emphysema or a stick-up artist from the Depression, there's nothing like it. And on this ranch: no prurient guesswork about slavery, but a whiff of the real thing. The owner was a stony little man who consented to chat with me only because I was accompanied by a fellow whose grazing rights he hoped to lease. My companion, curly-headed, under thirty but already a smoothie, was in a race for City Council, mending some fences as we toured. The smell of spring was in the air, and it was time to think of bringing in the cattle that had wintered beside the Gulf to mark them up and doctor them. The old man had four of his blacks standing around, and he was fussing like a spinning flywheel on a motor that hasn't been greased—that never *has* been greased. Not for a minute did he stop issuing orders and then countermanding them. "Hey, get the tractor going; no, kick it off; no, get it going again. It sounds funny, don't it—no, turn it off. Catch that sorrel—not the one-eye. Get the tractor going, catch him with that. No, turn it off, you can catch the sumbitch just walkin' at him." He kicked the tire of his pickup truck as we leaned against it and told another black to run and get the tire gauge. He squinted at the roof of his machinery shed—this was a corner of the ranch, not where he lived—was that rooftree busted? He thought somebody ought to climb up and look.

A range cow and her calf ran by the fence but swerved when he turned toward them, his gaze like a squirt of acid that festered for a moment, his hand bouncing just a little as he pointed. Though he had a friend visiting—a big-ribbed, frog-faced, impassive man retired from a career at one of the petrochemical plants, who did some poisoning for him as a hobby—he still burned openly with bitterness about the Civil War. He said his ranch had been larger then, and moved away from me until the only way I could hear what he was saying was to keep following him around the truck, sticking beside my City Council friend whose pasturage he wanted. In 1924, he said, a tidal wave and blizzard had killed two hundred cattle here; one hundred last winter had frozen to death. He buzzed in anger at the wolves as well—they bit his calves' tails off, or they would chase a calf until it panted and slash its tongue out so that it strangled on its blood—and at the rats in his oat bin, and at the vultures, which he said would flap around his cows when they were trying to drop a calf, scrapping with each other to do the honors on the after-birth until the mama strained herself in plunging at them and never was the same again. Scrambling to her feet, she might step on her infant inadvertently and cripple it. In the bayou bottom along one of his boundaries lived a drove of razorbacks, rooting in the mud and weeds. They were a remnant that had escaped his previous expeditions to kill them, and thinking of them, he decided he'd get his guns out tomorrow and go in there with all his niggers and clean them out—hang 'em up and cut 'em up. His fury made him hum.

Probably he was too old to really go and shoot the hogs; the federal government had forbidden him the use of the familiar wolf poisons—he'd have to send his friend to Mexico to buy some—and with the bad winter's dead cattle sprawled about, the vultures were increasing. His Negroes also were older men, the top hand the eldest, with a smile incised on his wrinkled face by so many decades that it had become a snarl. This fellow chuckled, every few words that he spoke, swaying with the dozen contradictory orders that came from Mr. Phil, but at the same time

he was as immune as a weathervane, never moving far unless the instructions were given again, and then renewed.
For me to have had to take orders from the man would
have been like torture with electrodes, but Em farmed with
them and never jerked as if they stung. Plum-black, a slim
knot of a fellow, he displayed his calluses to us when told to,
and had come to resemble his master a bit, as dogs are
said to. None of the young help could climb a windmill or
shoe a horse or mend a waterline like Em. Once he had
loaded eleven hundred cattle into stock cars in an hour
and three-quarters and sent the train highballing. He
mumbled that he "need a li'l money," grinning. Mr. Phil
laughed too and reached in a side pocket for his wallet,
which was fat and which he handled as men do their
scrotums when they soap themselves, and gave him two
one-dollar bills.

But it was the fizzing of Mr. Phil that got to me, not the
wages. He fizzed and his men twitched, and there was
nothing comic about it. He was grim, mischievous, puni-
tive, convinced that God had given him the land and the
people to work it with. I could envision him deliberating
on the question of whom to sell. We like to manufacture
metaphors and say that slavery is the bondage of a bad
love, or is the schoolboy who must grin along with his
tormentors at his own clumsiness. But slavery is not as
easy to re-create as that. Slavery was wiring that you
were hitched to: wired to the acid batteries of a crazy
brain.

Although he lived at the time of slavery, William Bartram had to go wandering among the Seminoles before he

recognized the utter anxiety in which slaves lived; and here I was wolfing in Texas to discover the same thing. My rancher was perpetually disgruntled, inspecting the blossoms on his peach tree for a blight, looking at his horses for a limp. He was so accustomed to the luxury of company to blow off to that he would only have noticed if he hadn't had four men dogging him to ring his comments on. He had them catch the sorrel horse, then let it go because he liked the white-socks better. No, grab the sorrel again. There were limits that the man had had to adjust to—he couldn't point to the top of a tree and send somebody up to check the soundness of a high branch— but his matter-of-factness was the worst of it.

Some of the "old boys," he said (that Texan conjunction of two fond words, "old" and "boy"), would get after a horse with a quirt until it could read and write, or at least read the brands. He said that when he went out bulldogging he used to tie the steers right where they lay with their heads down between their legs and their asses sticking up above the grass so that you'd spot them easily when you rode back at the end of the day. I could envision him tending the fire while the young stock was marked, frying the "prairie oysters" that his black cowboys tossed him and, to turn the clock back, some time during the hot afternoon pointing with a wink for his foreman's benefit at one of the blacks who had been feisty and having *his* balls in the frying pan too in half a minute.

In the early 1800s, jolly Jean Lafitte, the buccaneer of Louisiana and Galveston Island, used to sell the slaves that he was pirating to the settlers at a dollar a pound.

His lieutenants, the Berthoud brothers, would race in longboats with slave crews and with a pistol nip a snip off someone's ear if he broke the stroke. Phil said that fifty years after the import business in slaves had been proscribed, bootlegged blacks were still being spirited into the estuary of the Sabine River here and auctioned on its banks. "We put their first clothes on them."

As I left Texas for Louisiana and New York again, an old gaunt black man hobbled out onto a desolate section of the superhighway, newly opened to traffic, in order to hitchhike. There was no exit close by, and by his breathless manner I could see it was some kind of an emergency for him. He must have been up in his seventies, and with a desperately obeisant gesture he doffed his floppy hat, waved it and held it out, almost blindly, as if asking alms from the gods in the sky. It was too stark and sudden for me, as naked as slavery. I had been dreaming the night before of several red foxes that were struggling in a steel trap, and me clubbing them, each fox that had been beaten dead reviving to struggle and be clubbed again. I was wondering about myself, and why it was that though the people I most cared about were women, the only people whom I really wrote about were men. I was whizzing by at eighty miles an hour, frantically lonely, singing in my loudest bathroom voice again, "God is good, God is great!" and didn't have sufficient time to react with anything beyond astonishment to what to a white Southerner would have seemed only a very plain and homey gesture of beseechment.

NINE SMALL
(LITERARY)
TRUTHS

Afew home truths about writing bear repeating from time to time.

1) All good writers are good. That is, for example, you and I might argue out the merits of Walker Percy's books and William Styron's, one championing Percy as a Southern writer, the other Styron, but with practitioners of that caliber, the championing should be the point of it.

2) Nevertheless, whatever Percy's worth vis-à-vis Styron's, there is no justice in the disparity between how much mentioned the two names are. The arts are cruel in regard to rewards—cruelest, of course, to the earnest author who is not so good, because however ineptly he writes, he perhaps *reads* just as well and has the same aspirations as the better fellow. Writers do want to become famous. At parties famous writers hang out together, often asking for a guest list before agreeing to go. Although the ones to whom fame came late seem to enjoy it more, that's only because they didn't have it to enjoy before. Either way, they generally arrive at their maturity and get whatever

is coming to them like the mythical elected official who "owes nothing to anybody." One magazine or another may have been buying their work, they may have had advisers, and some kind soul found them a teaching job or fellowship at some point, but essentially they reached their level of competence without anybody's assistance at all.

3) There are writers' writers and readers' writers, and though each group is inclined to envy the other, the writers' writers envy the readers' writers more and cross over if they find that they can. After all, writers want to be read.

4) Writing is nearly as taxing as a vocation as it is as a craft. Among the arts, it calls for an analytic intelligence directed to the specifics of the human dilemma, and hence makes of its cadre a jittery lot. The toll in nervous excesses is substantial, and perhaps the cause of the affection which editors and literary agents display in speaking of their clients. Although an editor or agent stands to profit from part of the sympathy he gives, there are others whose motives are simply enthusiastic, such as Galen Williams, whose Poets and Writers group makes young poets feel less lonely nationwide, and Patrick Hynan, a Canadian broadcaster who goes around getting on tape the voices of neglected veterans ranging from Nelson Algren to Archibald MacLeish.

5) Writers are soreheads—each other's chief hexers— and hopelessly recidivistic in this regard. Chewing their beards, baleful of eye, most writers will send up a cluster of ack-ack and barrage balloons when they detect a rival.

Though this proclivity for spite can be exaggerated (a well-known writer I know complains that a less successful friend apparently has it in for him, yet when you ask around it turns out he has been sleeping with his old buddy's wife), why do they bad-mouth and poor-mouth at all? They poor-mouth because they feel poor. Even if they're not, they have lived by their wits, giddy from the brinkmanship. The man cheered early on is not usually so touched by luck in middle age, and the man praised in his ripe years has probably been scarred by the silence that greeted his first books. They bad-mouth each other because they feel terribly isolated a good deal of the time, alone all day, with eventual failure built into the effort. A new author will sleep with his first book under the bedclothes with him after it arrives in the mail, but his last book, as likely as not, he'll loathe as another bad job, and put it aside, its reviews unread. Novelists start writing journalism, plays or children's books, and journalists begin novels, and even if the fellow still feels his talent growing stronger, he realizes the process is not fast enough—knows the incalculable wattage of Chekhov, knows, too, the difference between a Fanny Hill and Moll Flanders, but in a dozen years he couldn't hope even to write a *Fanny Hill*.

6) Writers live for their work and find that, good or bad, their work becomes their rod and staff. Notwithstanding the temptation of jealousy, most do possess the gift of friendship with other writers: some with those who are older, some with the young and struggling (not necessarily the same individuals who were themselves once

befriended by the influential and old). Many are able to
make friends with their contemporaries as well. There are
definably foul- but not fair-weather friends, and friends
for fair but not foul weather. Apart from friendship, loose
literary alliances exist that are not primarily political, as
in the thirties when Communists and social democrats
warred, but casual and "ethnic"—i.e., women or Texans
together. It isn't too serious, and in the apportioning of
awards fine things may happen, flying in the face of the
adage that it's not what but whom you know. As among
professional soldiers, quarter will be given to a limping
warrior who has for years risked life and limb, regardless
of which side of any particular faction he happened to be
on.

7) It has been said that writers of commentary, as
opposed to fiction, wish either to be feared or loved, and
that a division may be drawn among them in this respect.
Just as often the division appears within the writer himself, who in the morning wants to be feared and in
the afternoon wants to be loved. In either case the
effects operate by old laws. He discovers that wanting to
be loved is awfully time-consuming; gaining an inside
track winds up being not much use politically if he does
not produce a body of work. On the other hand, if he
makes himself feared, then he must reckon with the time-
honored toe-stubber that whoever lives by the sword is
going to die impaled. Only a few identifiable critics write
to be feared, and I am oddly moved by them when I see
them in the flesh, although the image of their predeces-

sors, such as Alexander Woollcott, never appealed to me. I find, in other words, that they are not mere dictatorial literary bullies but injured people, vividly discomforted in the world—so uncomfortable, indeed, that they don't want the rest of us to be at our ease. They are as impartial as their compulsion permits, and in the absence of a dependable commentator like Edmund Wilson, who read almost everything by almost everybody of his time, the only critics more convincing are those who write not from discomfiture or a craving for love, but *out of* love, or at least the hope and wish to love.

8) Some writers write fast, others slow. We tend to read the fast writers swiftly and the slow authors more deliberately, if we are attuned to the book, because the manner of composition communicates itself to us. Especially in fiction, no undue importance should be attached to the mathematics of this. The slower performers like to boast about how they dragged and steamed, while the speedster prides himself on the rush of his words, although in fact he probably rewrote just as much during the period when he was mulling over his book before beginning it. If not, he has developed by the process of writing several similar books instead of several successive drafts of the same book.

9) Most writers are handed at least one free throw. They stumble on a scene that suits them—as Martin Russ did when he captured the Korean War in *The Thirty-eighth Parallel*. They blunder on the opportunity to write about their dead mothers and fathers too, for instance, dis-

covering to their surprise that they can hardly help doing it well. Otherwise, some first-rate writers resemble those appealing movie actors who finally are only able to portray themselves. If they are artful, that can be enough, but every reader is on the watch, grateful for more.

DOGS,

AND THE TUG

OF LIFE

It used to be that you could
tell just about how poor a family was by how many dogs
they had. If they had one, they were probably doing all
right. It was only American to keep a dog to represent
the family's interests in the intrigues of the back alley;
not to have a dog at all would be like not acknowledging
one's poor relations. Two dogs meant that the couple were
dog lovers, with growing children, but still might be members of the middle class. But if a citizen kept three, you
could begin to suspect he didn't own much else. Four or
five irrefutably marked the household as poor folk, whose
yard was also full of broken cars cannibalized for parts.
The father worked not much, fancied himself a hunter;
the mother's teeth were black. And an old bachelor living
in a shack might possibly have even more, but you knew
that if one of them, chasing a moth, didn't upset his oil
lamp some night and burn him up, he'd fetch up in the
poorhouse soon, with the dogs shot. Nobody got poor
feeding a bunch of dogs, needless to say, because the

more dogs a man had, the less he fed them. Foraging as a pack, they led an existence of their own, but served as evidence that life was awfully lonesome for him and getting out of hand. If a dog really becomes a man's best friend his situation is desperate.

That dogs, low-comedy confederates of small children and ragged bachelors, should have turned into an emblem of having made it to the middle class—like the hibachi, like golf clubs and a second car—seems at the very least incongruous. Puppies which in the country you would have to carry in a box to the church fair to give away are bringing seventy-five dollars apiece in some of the pet stores, although in fact dogs are in such oversupply that one hundred and fifty thousand are running wild in New York City alone.

There is another line of tradition about dogs, however. Show dogs, toy dogs, foxhounds for formal hunts, Doberman guard dogs, bulldogs as ugly as a queen's dwarf. An aristocratic Spanish lady once informed me that when she visits her Andalusian estate each fall the mastiffs rush out and fawn about her but would tear to pieces any of the servants who have accompanied her from Madrid. In Mississippi it was illegal for a slave owner to permit his slaves to have a dog, just as it was to teach them how to read. A "negro dog" was a hound trained by a bounty hunter to ignore the possums, raccoons, hogs and deer in the woods that other dogs were supposed to chase, and trail and tree a runaway. The planters themselves, for whom hunting was a principal recreation, whooped it up when a man unexpectedly became their quarry. They caught each other's slaves and would often sit back and let the dogs do the punishing. Bennet H. Barrow of West Feliciana Parish in Louisiana, a rather moderate and representative plantation owner, recounted in his diary of the 1840s, among several similar incidents, this for November 11, 1845: In "5 minutes had him up & a going, And never in my life did I ever see as excited beings as R & myself, ran ½ miles & caught him dogs soon tore him naked, took him Home Before the other negro(es) at dark & made the dogs give him another over hauling." Only recently in Louisiana I heard what happened to two Negroes who happened to be fishing in a bayou off the Blind River, where four white men with a shotgun felt like fishing alone. One was forced to pretend to be a scampering coon and shinny up a telephone pole and hang there till he fell, while the other impersonated a baying, bounding hound.

Such memories are not easy to shed, particularly since childhood, the time when people can best acquire a comradeship with animals, is also when they are likely to pick up their parents' fears. A friend of mine hunts quail by jeep in Texas with a millionaire who brings along forty bird dogs, which he deploys in eight platoons that spell each other off. Another friend though, will grow apprehensive at a dinner party if the host lets a dog loose in the room. The toothy, mysterious creature lies dreaming on the carpet, its paws pulsing, its eyelids open, the nictitating membranes twitching; how can he be certain it won't suddenly jump up and attack his legs under the table? Among Eastern European Jews, possession of a dog was associated with the hard-drinking *goyishe* peasantry, traditional antagonists, or else with the gentry, and many carried this dislike to the New World. An immigrant fleeing a potato famine or the hunger of Calabria might be no more equipped with the familiar British-German partiality to dogs—a failing which a few rugged decades in a great city's slums would not necessarily mend. The city had urbanized plenty of native farmers' sons as well, and so it came about that what to rural America had been the humblest, most natural amenity—friendship with a dog —has been transmogrified into a piece of the jigsaw of moving to the suburbs: there to cook outdoors, another bit of absurdity to the old countryman, whose toilet was outdoors but who was pleased to be able to cook and eat his meals inside the house.

There are an estimated forty million dogs in the United States (nearly two for every cat). Thirty-seven thousand of them are being destroyed in humane institutions every day, a figure which indicates that many more are in trouble. Dogs are hierarchal beasts, with several million years of submission to the structure of a wolf pack in their breeding. This explains why the Spanish lady's mastiffs can distinguish immediately between the mistress and her retainers, and why it is about as likely that one of the other guests at the dinner party will attack my friend's legs under the table as that the host's dog will, once it has accepted his presence in the room as proper. Dogs need leadership, however; they seek it, and when it's not forthcoming quickly fall into difficulties in a world where they can no longer provide their own.

"Dog" is "God" spelled backwards—one might say, way

backwards. There's "a dog's life," "dog days," "dog-sick," "dog-tired," "dog-cheap," "dog-eared," "doghouse," and "dogs" meaning villains or feet. Whereas a wolf's stamina was measured in part by how long he could go without water, a dog's is becoming a matter of how long he can *hold* his water. He retrieves a rubber ball instead of coursing deer, chases a broom instead of hunting marmots. His is the lowest form of citizenship: that tug of life at the end of the leash is like the tug at the end of a fishing pole, and then one doesn't have to kill it. On stubby, amputated-looking feet he leads his life, which if we glance at it attentively is a kind of cutout of our own, all the more so for being riskier and shorter. Bam! A member of the family is dead on the highway, as we expected he would be, and we just cart him to the dump and look for a new pup.

Simply the notion that he lives on four legs instead of two has come to seem astonishing—like a goat or cow wearing horns on its head. And of course to keep a dog is a way of attempting to bring nature back. The primitive hunter's intimacy, telepathy, with the animals he sought, surprising them at their meals and in their beds, then stripping them of their warm coats to expose a frame so like our own, is all but lost. Sport hunters, especially the older ones, retain a little of it still; and naturalists who have made up their minds not to kill wild animals nevertheless appear to empathize primarily with the predators at first, as a look at the tigers, bears, wolves, mountain lions on the project list of an organization such as the World Wildlife Fund will show. This is as it should be, these creatures

246

having suffered from our brotherly envy before. But in order to really enjoy a dog, one doesn't merely try to train him to be semihuman. The point of it is to open oneself to the possibility of becoming partly a dog (after all, there are plenty of sub- or semi-human beings around whom we don't wish to adopt). One wants to rediscover the commonality of animal and man—to see an animal eat and sleep that hasn't forgotten how to enjoy doing such things—and the directness of its loyalty.

The trouble with the current emphasis on preserving "endangered species" is that, however beneficial to wildlife the campaign works out to be, it makes all animals seem like museum pieces, worth saving for sentimental considerations and as figures of speech (to "shoot a sitting duck"), but as a practical matter already dead and gone. On the contrary, some animals are flourishing. In 1910 half a million deer lived in the United States, in 1960 seven million, in 1970 sixteen million. What has happened is that now that we don't eat them we have lost that close interest.

Wolf behavior prepared dogs remarkably for life with human beings. So complete and complicated was the potential that it was only a logical next step for them to quit their packs in favor of the heady, hopeless task of trying to keep pace with our own community development. The contortions of fawning and obeisance which render group adjustment possible among such otherwise forceful fighters—sometimes humping the inferior members into the shape of hyenas—are what squeezes them past our tantrums, too. Though battling within the pack is mostly accomplished with body checks that do no damage, a subordinate wolf bitch is likely to remain so in awe of the leader that she will cringe and sit on her tail in response to his amorous advances, until his female co-equal has had a chance to notice and dash over and redirect his attention. Altogether, he is kept so busy asserting his dominance that this top-ranked female may not be bred by him, finally, but by the male which occupies the second rung. Being breadwinners, dominant wolves feed first and best, just as we do, so that to eat our scraps and leavings strikes a dog as normal procedure. Nevertheless, a wolf puppy up to eight months old is favored at a kill, and when smaller can extract a meal from any pack member—uncles and aunts as well as parents—by nosing the lips of the adult until it regurgitates a share of what it's had. The care of the litter is so much a communal endeavor that the benign sort of role we expect dogs to play within our own families toward children not biologically theirs comes naturally to them.

For dogs and wolves the tail serves as a semaphore of mood and social code, but dogs carry their tails higher than wolves do, as a rule, which is appropriate, since the excess spirits that used to go into lengthy hunts now have no other outlet than backyard negotiating. In addition to an epistolary anal gland, whose message-carrying function has not yet been defined, the anus itself, or stool when sniffed, conveys how well the animal has been eating—in effect, its income bracket—although most dog foods are sorrily monotonous compared to the hundreds of tastes a wolf encounters, perhaps dozens within the carcass of a single moose. We can speculate on a dog's powers of taste because its olfactory area is proportionately fourteen times larger than a man's, its sense of smell at least a hundred times as keen.

The way in which a dog presents his anus and genitals for inspection indicates the hierarchal position that he aspires to, and other dogs who sniff his genitals are apprised of his sexual condition. From his urine they can undoubtedly distinguish age, build, state of sexual activity and general health, even hours after he's passed by. Male dogs dislike running out of urine, as though an element of potency were involved, and try to save a little; they prefer not to use a scent post again until another dog has urinated there, the first delight and duty of the ritual being to stake out a territory, so that when they are walked hurriedly in the city it is a disappointment to them. The search is also sexual, because bitches in heat post notices about. In the woods a dog will mark his drinking places, and watermark a rabbit's trail after chasing it, as if to notify the next predator that happens by exactly who it was that put such a whiff of fear into the rabbit's scent. Similarly, he squirts the tracks of bobcats and of skunks with an aloof air unlike his brisk and cheery manner of branding another dog's or fox's trail, and if he is in a position to do so, will defecate excitedly on a bear run, leaving behind his best effort, which no doubt he hopes will strike the bear as a bombshell.

The chief complaint people lodge against dogs is their extraordinary stress upon lifting the leg and moving the bowels. Scatology did take up some of the slack for them when they left behind the entertainments of the forest. The forms of territoriality replaced the substance. But apart from that, a special zest for life is characteristic of dogs and wolves—in hunting, eating, relieving themselves, in punctiliously maintaining a home territory, a pecking order and a love life, and educating the resulting pups. They grin and grimace and scrawl graffiti with their piss. A lot of inherent strategy goes into these activities: the way wolves spell each other off, both when hunting and in their governess duties around the den, and often "consult" as a pack with noses together and tails wagging before flying in to make a kill. (Tigers, leopards, house cats base their social relations instead upon what ethologists call "mutual avoidance.") The nose is a dog's main instrument of discovery, corresponding to our eyes, and so it is that he is seldom offended by organic smells, such as putrefaction, and sniffs intently for the details of illness, gum bleeding and diet in his master and his fellows, and for the story told by scats, not closing off the avenue for any reason—just as we rarely shut our eyes against new information, even the tragic or unpleasant kind.

Though dogs don't see as sharply as they smell, trainers usually rely on hand signals to instruct them, and most firsthand communication in a wolf pack also seems to be visual—by the expressions of the face, by body english and the cant of the tail. A dominant wolf squares his mouth, stares at and "rides up" on an inferior, standing with his front legs on its back, or will pretend to stalk it, creeping along, taking its muzzle in his mouth, and performing nearly all of the other discriminatory pranks and practices familiar to anybody who has a dog. In fact, what's funny is to watch a homely mutt as tiny as a shoe-box spin through the rigmarole which a whole series of observers in the wilderness have gone to great pains to document for wolves.

Dogs proffer their rear ends to each other in an intimidating fashion, but when they examine the region of the head it is a friendlier gesture, a snuffling between pals. One of them may come across a telltale bone fragment caught in the other's fur, together with a bit of mud to give away the location of bigger bones. On the same impulse, wolves and free-running dogs will sniff a wanderer's toes to find out where he has been roaming. They fondle and propitiate with their mouths also, and lovers groom each other's fur with tongues and teeth adept as hands. A bitch wolf's period in heat includes a week of preliminary behavior and maybe two weeks of receptivity—among animals, exceptionally long. Each actual copulative tie lasts twenty minutes or a half an hour, which again may help to instill affection. Wolves sometimes begin choosing a mate as early as the age of one, almost a year before they are ready to breed. Dogs mature sexually a good deal earlier, and arrive in heat twice a year instead of once—at any season instead of only in midwinter, like a wolf, whose pups' arrival must be scheduled unfailingly for spring. Dogs have not retained much responsibility for raising their young, and the summertime is just as perilous as winter for them because, apart from the whimsy of their owners, who put so many of them to sleep, their nemesis is the automobile. Like scatology, sex helps fill the gulf of what is gone.

The scientist David Mech has pointed out how like the posture of a wolf with a nosehold on a moose (as other wolves attack its hams) are the antics of a puppy playing tug-of-war at the end of a towel. Anybody watching a dog's exuberance as it samples bites of long grass beside a brook, or pounds into a meadow bristling with the odors of woodchucks, snowshoe rabbits, grouse, a doe and buck, field mice up on the seedheads of the weeds, kangaroo mice jumping, chipmunks whistling, weasels and shrews on the hunt, a plunging fox, a porcupine couched in a tree, perhaps can begin to imagine the variety of excitements under the sky that his ancestors relinquished in order to move indoors with us. He'll lie down with a lamb to please us, but as he sniffs its haunches, surely he must remember atavistically that this is where he'd start to munch.

There is poignancy in the predicament of a great many animals: as in the simple observation which students of the California condor have made that this huge, most endangered bird prefers the carrion meat of its old standby, the deer, to all the dead cows, sheep, horses and other substitutes it sees from above, sprawled about. Animals are stylized characters in a kind of old saga—stylized because even the most acute of them have little leeway as they play out their parts. (*Rabbits*, for example, I find terribly affecting, imprisoned in their hop.) And as we drift away from any cognizance of them, we sacrifice some of the intricacy and grandeur of life. Having already lost so much, we are hardly aware of what remains, but to a primitive snatched forward from an earlier existence it might seem as if we had surrendered a richness comparable to all the tapestries of childhood. Since this is a matter of the imagination as well as of animal demographics, no Noah projects, no bionomic discoveries on the few sanctuaries that have been established are going to reverse the swing. The very specialists in the forefront of finding out how animals behave, when one meets them, appear to be no more intrigued than any ordinary Indian was.

But we continue to need—as aborigines did, as children do—a parade of morality tales which are more concise than those that politics, for instance, later provides. So we've had Aesop's and medieval and modern fables about the grasshopper and the ant, the tiger and Little Black Sambo, the wolf and the three pigs, Br'er Rabbit and Br'er Bear, Goldilocks and her three bears, Pooh Bear, Babar and the rhinos, Walt Disney's animals, and assorted humbler scary bats, fat hippos, funny frogs and eager beavers. Children have a passion for clean, universal definitions, and so it is that animals have gone with children's literature as Latin has with religion. Through them they first encountered death, birth, their own maternal feelings, the gap between beauty and cleverness, or speed and good intentions. The animal kingdom boasted the powerful lion, the mothering goose, the watchful owl, the tardy tortoise, Chicken Little, real-life dogs that treasure bones, and mink that grow posh pelts from eating crawfish and mussels.

In the cartoons of two or three decades ago, Mouse doesn't get along with Cat because Cat must catch Mouse or miss his supper. Dog, on the other hand, detests Cat for no such rational reason, only the capricious fact that dogs don't dote on cats. Animal stories are bounded, yet enhanced, by each creature's familiar lineaments, just as a parable about a prince and peasant, a duchess and a milk-maid, a blacksmith and a fisherman, would be. Typecasting, like the roll of a metered ode, adds resonance and dignity, summoning up all of the walruses and hedgehogs that went before: the shrewd image of Br'er Rabbit to assist his suburban relative Bugs Bunny behind the scenes. But now, in order to present a tale about the contest between two thieving crows and a scarecrow, the storyteller would need to start by explaining that once upon a time crows used to eat a farmer's corn if he didn't defend it with a mock man pinned together from old clothes. Crows are having a hard go of it and may soon receive game-bird protection.

One way childhood is changing, therefore, is that the nonhuman figures—"Wild Things" or puppet monsters—constructed by the best of the new artificers, like Maurice Sendak or the *Sesame Street* writers, are distinctly humanoid, ballooned out of faces, torsos met on the subway. The televised character Big Bird does not resemble a bird the way Bugs Bunny remained a rabbit—though already he was less so than Br'er or Peter Rabbit. Big Bird's personality, her confusion, haven't the faintest connection to an ostrich's. Lest she be confused with an ostrich, her voice has been slotted unmistakably toward the prosaic. Dr. Seuss did transitional composites of worldwide fauna, but these new shapes—a beanbag like the *Sesame Street* Grouch or Cookie Monster or Herry Monster, and the floral creations in books—have been conceived practically from scratch by the artist ("in the night kitchen," to use a Sendak phrase), and not transferred from the existing caricatures of nature. In their conversational conflicts they offer him a fresh start, which may be a valuable commodity, whereas if he were dealing with an alligator, it would, while giving him an old-fashioned boost in the traditional manner, at the same time box him in. A chap called Alligator, with that fat snout and tail, cannot squirm free of the solidity of actual alligators. Either it must stay a heavyweight or else play on the sternness of reality by swinging over to impersonate a cream puff and a Ferdinand.

Though animal programs on television are popular, what with the wave of nostalgia and "ecology" in the country, we can generally say about the animal kingdom, "The King is dead, long live the King." Certainly the talent has moved elsewhere. Those bulbous Wild Things and slant-mouthed beanbag puppets derived from the denizens of Broadway—an argumentative night news vendor, a lady on a traffic island—have grasped their own destinies, as characters on the make are likely to. It was inevitable they would. There may be a shakedown to remove the elements that would be too bookish for children's literature in other hands, and another shakedown because these first innovators have been more city-oriented than suburban. New authors will shift the character sources away from Broadway and the subway and the ghetto, but the basic switch has already been accomplished—from the ancient juxtaposition of people, animals, and dreams blending the two, to people and monsters that grow solely out of people by way of dreams.

Which leaves us in the suburbs, with dogs as a last link. Cats are too independent to care, but dogs are in an unenviable position, they hang so much upon our good opinion. We are coming to *have* no opinion; we don't pay enough attention to form an opinion. Though they admire us, are thrilled by us, heroize us, we regard them as a hobby or a status symbol, like a tennis racquet, and substitute leash laws for leadership—expect them not simply to learn English but to grow hands, because their beastly paws seem stranger to us every year. If they try to fondle us with their handyjack mouths, we read it as a bite; and like used cars, they are disposed of when the family relocates, changes its "bag," or in the scurry of divorce. The first reason people kept a dog was to acquire an ally on the hunt, a friend at night. Then it was to maintain an avenue to animality, as our own nearness began to recede. But as we lose our awareness of all animals, dogs are becoming a bridge to nowhere. We can only pity their fate.

OTHER
LIVES

Often there seems to be a
playfulness to wise people, as if either their equanimity
has as its source this playfulness or the playfulness flows
from the equanimity; and they can persuade other people
who are in a state of agitation to calm down and manage
a smile. If they believe in God and an afterlife, then the
parts of life we are not responsible for are naturally rather
a game. If they don't believe, they find that generally it
is more sensible to be amused than miserable. But what
used to surprise me and make me a good deal less judging
of people was to realize how vulnerable nearly all of them
are, including these grown-up types. Unless he craves to
straddle the world, there may be just a kernel of basic
reassurance that each person needs. He needs some friends,
some modest success in love or love life, a reasonable
sense of accomplishment in the work that he does, and a
home. Yet these benefits, in competition, are not so easily
obtained. If our needs seem relatively simple, the psyches
with which and the circumstances from which we must

win satisfaction are not, and we live a long while, besides, seldom able to rest on our laurels.

So one discovers that everybody's equilibrium is surprisingly shaky, that you can't with impunity criticize someone, and that if you do criticize him you may rattle him more than you had intended. More to the point, though, I began to grasp that snap judgments are incomplete, unjust, that the complex of emotion and difficulty in which another man lives cannot be quickly ascertained. Of course, the glory and luck of it is that running counter to all that shakiness is a resilience: you can't shake up the fellow for long. Most of us have a way of riding out assaults or disappointments of even the toughest variety, an animal salubrity that somehow takes over and that we trust in, that makes us begin to grin a little again after a night's sleep, a long walk in the sunshine, a good meal or two.

The great leveler nowadays is divorce; almost everybody thinks about it, whether because we expect to be happy all the time—daily, weekly—or because we want the smell of brimstone in lives made too affluent and easy. Maybe some of us will end up back with the same wives and husbands again at the end of our lives (we sometimes hope so), but in the meantime it's as if marriage had become a chancy, grim, modern experiment instead of an ancient institution. *We have other lives to lead,* we say to ourselves, casting about for more freedom or erotic sizzle, more simplicity, leisure, "integrity" at work, or money, or whatever. Physiologically men reach their sexual peak at nineteen, an appropriate age for their original life span of thirty years, but now they have forty more years to go, and the expectation is that every year should be terribly straightforward or terribly crowded in every respect. To be original is to be lonely, we've always been told, and for that reason, too, we may feel the need for some form of hazard to enter our lives, especially if it was not in our diet when we were young. Many divorces are not really the result of irreparable injury but involve, instead, a desire on the part of the man or woman to shatter the setup, start out from scratch alone, and make life work for them all over again. They want the risk of disaster, want to touch bottom, see where bottom is, and, coming up, to breathe the air with relief and relish again.

It's not easy. The public effort to look harmonious may help hold some couples together. After sitting in silence going to a party, they will hold hands in the taxi when they come home; they make love rarely, but do so with pleasure if they have company staying over. Moreover, some of their differences are disconcertingly homely ones. She wants to sell the house, he wants to keep it, and they disagree about the children's school. He resents the fact that she got herself pregnant "accidentally" for each of the children, but she is sick and tired of battling his timidity, which, among other things, would have meant that he'd never have had any children at all if she hadn't taken matters in hand. He resents almost as a betrayal her quick abandonment of most of the sex games—what she calls "Krafft-Ebbing" now—that so pleased him during their courtship and drew him on, but she is tired of holding him to a maturity that should befit the head of a household; it doesn't seem to come naturally to him. Bachelors fall into two types, as she sees them—the "glassies," who reflect back what they encounter, and the thickset, blocked, sad fellows, to whom passivity is a pain and a blight—and he probably would have been one of the latter if she hadn't turned up, had their first child and settled down into family life, exchanging her rakish black boots for shoes. She wants to go to Europe this summer, whereas he wants to bask at the beach. She thinks he treats his mother and father badly and that his behavior in their own fights is a continuation of hangups he has with them, but he makes no bones at all about his contention that her affection for *her* parents is livelier than what she feels for him, that even her preoccupation with motherhood is partly an attempt to give to the world her mother all over again.

They're at swords' points; grotesqueries come to the fore. He carries a portable radio everywhere, even to the dinner table, the bathroom, and she constantly plays with the dog. He's sick of the hack of her nervous cough and she of his scratching his ass. In bed, when they argue late into the night or lie rigid, unable to speak, she crosses her arms on her chest and he holds his balls as if to keep them intact for life later on. Apprehension and exhaustion make them postpone separating, but they take to fighting via notes left in prominent spots about the house, bulletins to be read in silence and answered by the same method, which cuts down the talk. Yet neither really wants this disaster; their nerves and their stomachs beg them to have a care.

For a poor boy, just earning a lot of money used to be plenty. Now moneymaking is seldom sufficient—*we have other lives to lead.* On the contrary, the higher the wages, the more wildcat strikes there are; a malaise afflicts the assembly lines. It's their time off that people are concerned with. Hitchhiking has had a new vogue for its dramatization of rootlessness, and a good many young men and women brought up comfortably in the suburbs have plunged into bucolic living, the men immediately confronting the extraordinary question of whether or not they could build a house for themselves. To do so seemed essential to them, and a surprising proportion did manage somehow. As one visits among the communes, one finds the woods full of houses—sheepherders' cabins, Japanese hutches, alpine chalets, airy, belvedered, summery bowers —that often are empty. The fellow, hastily beginning the job, worrying about that formidable scatter of sawmill lumber—the footing and sills and studs and siding—forgot to think about locating water, or built uphill from his spring. Or maybe the site is so woodsy-lovely that his girlfriend finds it frightening at night; they're sleeping instead in a Volkswagen van parked next to the central farmhouse. Isolated shacks dispersed about may have come to seem in conflict with the overall experiment in living. Or perhaps the builders merely moved on, leaving these homes like dated bomb shelters.

Some communes are for homesteading, others are rest homes or pleasure domes. Some are loose neighborly arrangements not unlike pioneer settlements where the people pitched in to help one another; others have a religiosity about them, though it may rather smack of the Children's Crusade. In Vermont, close by the subsistence existence that with some difficulty can still be achieved—outhouse, staked pig—is the fact of Boston or New York a few hours away. Even though the choice of living this way has been deliberate, a communard would have to be unusual to shut himself up on a mountain slope as if the contemporary world didn't exist at all. So these people make trips out, dipping into the maelstrom of the city every few months, working locally in town if they need cash, a rhythm that can be precise. Movies, restaurants, traffic, then home to a brook they can drink from: silence, noise, silence and noise.

Because it's a bad time for ideology, the communes are fading in favor of families who live private lives on a separate but cooperative basis. The problem remains that a place where land is cheap enough for the simple life is also a depressed area, where even the natives don't find much work, and so the women tend to do better than the men as the months become years. Not feeling obliged to come up with the mortgage money, the women set about doing what they might do anywhere—taking care of the kids, being ameliorative, homemaking. Particularly if they are the earth-mother sort to begin with, they thrive, while the men are dishwashers during the tourist season or carpenters or mechanics or set up a bakery, do leatherwork, carve salad bowls, drive a truck, until the limitations to earning a living in such a parched economy may come to seem not worth the candle.

I don't believe this rural activity is only a footnote to

the divisiveness of the Vietnam war. People are going to keep choosing a manner of living to suit themselves, and there are going to be different ways: we forget what miracles we are. On summer holidays some of the long-haired couples and communes in my town in Vermont get together for a big softball game, everybody contributing food for the meal that follows. The lush grass is high except where they've knocked it down, the outfield is full of extra fielders, and each team tries to run up the score. Watching the playing, the smiles people wear as they swing, I think it must be as gleeful a time as any, these late twenties that most of them are in. Sometimes I feel as though I'm looking at snapshots taken today of one or another of them, young, happy, at a kind of peak, on the best afternoon of their twenty-eighth summer. It's so American a scene that nearly everyone must be repre-sented here, the lank hair only a disguise. I wonder where they will be, what will have happened to them, what changes their faces will show in twenty-eight more. Smil-ing in the sun, a girl takes a strong swing, and I feel per-haps some of the same painful tenderness she herself would feel years from now, holding pictures from today in her hands, pictures such as old men and women will show you to indicate that they too were graceful once and had happy times.

Afterwards, when the crowd is gone, my friend who owns the ballfield calls in his herd of goats for milking. "Goatee! Goatee!" The goats with their bland farmer faces run in a bevy of white bobbing heads, mild-looking. The unfinished new barn is a competent cross-hatch of joists and roof beams, taller than it will seem when it is completed. We are friends because recently we walked forty-five miles together, cooking over wispy fires, eating from the same pot, hunching under a canvas fly in the rain. He is so well settled here after eight years that it took me almost the whole hike to see him in the other guise that I always look for: what he would have been like if he hadn't left New York City. Finally, in the rain when he was tired, I did recognize the New York face he would have worn, and it was darkly confused and sad. Often behind the communard's veil of hair one sees a man who is just marking time, sliding past forks in the road that he should take, but here was my friend, with his fields and his garden and goats, in the midst of life.

During the Black Power period of the late 1960s in New York City, one babysitter who came to our apartment looked at our baby's blond head, and when she thought that they were alone, said to her, "How would you like to be thrown out the window?" But another babysitter caught my hand when I paid her and tried to kiss it and lay it against her cheek, while her knees bent as if she were going to kneel—this not "camp," you understand; her boyfriend was a white policeman, and it was actually what she most wished to do. There is no accounting for individuality. Hairdressers at the same time were costuming themselves as if for service under the Jolly Roger, with hanging the penalty if they were caught. Their savage mustaches would have fit them to ride with a bandit band in the massifs of Afghanistan.

In New York if I go out my door and turn left I'm at the federal holding penitentiary almost immediately. Loudspeakers, guards with carbines, men in fetters taking a last look at the street before being led inside. There are attorneys, and the rigmarole of bread deliveries, and visiting wives, mothers and babies—"ten years!" in the snatches of conversation. It's said not to be a harsh place and probably would not have the facilities to handle much trouble, in any case. The guards who do look like ugly customers are the out-of-staters from prisons like Lewisburg who have driven in vans to transport the sentenced prisoners for a longer stay. They play with their chains as they wait—long waist and leg chains.

Turning right on the street, I'm soon at a drug peddlers' location, a slithy spot at midnight, where two dozen trucks are kept closely parked in a narrow lot and the very moonlight is blocked off by railroad tracks running above. Over by a single bulb at the far corner a mechanic, as a cover, is leaning into an engine, making some repairs, while the sellers, several of them, pace in and out between the tight trucks, quickly disappearing in the darkness to reappear at another spot. A series of Dickensian starvelings scutter up, each one palavering furtively and then moving off, while other addicts await their turn in the gloomy doorways down the block. They are mostly so thin that they remind me of the poverty of another continent, casting desolate-looking faces backward as they come, to see whether anybody is following them. But some drive up and park; and there's a courier service for wholesale deals, because every few minutes an off-duty taxi

265

swings slowly past to make a pickup—if the cabbie is scared he keeps going around the block until one of the peddlers whistles at him. It's a perfect maze, and if all the people transacting business in an evening were scooped up, they would fill the federal detention headquarters. Some will find themselves there rapidly enough anyway. For them it is only a step from being free to being nabbed. They've already largely been nabbed.

The foghorns of this stretch of the waterfront, carried through the window, cause a slippage of resolve in me, just as they must work to demoralize the prisoners and peddlers and addicts nearby—we have other lives to lead. I'm not so sure I know what is permanent any more, although as recently as a year or two ago I thought that I did. The stars, the flowers, and so on—genes, mountains, and even the sore points of love. Picking at the heaps of raspberries growing up from the ruins of an old barn—sweet from the manuring of twenty years—I'd find a quietude in that. And our choreography, too, outlives us. A porcupine pushes its head around the corner of the house, and with weak bulging eyes cautiously sits up on its hindquarters before venturing onto the lawn. Porcupines chew holes in houses, so I slide inside for my gun. When my dog sees me loading he thinks his time may have come. He knows there is no escape, if so, having seen other men shoot other dogs, and he cringes as our eyes meet. The porcupine, which had retreated alongside the house, heads for the woods when I reappear, its waddle suddenly transformed into a flight for life. It is a primitive animal that when wounded still only waddles, cannot limp, but die it does, holding its wound with one hand and bracing itself with the other, sighing as a person would. Yet during this sad episode I've felt larger, quicker, hardly myself, augmented as though by the fact that each of us has moved along tracks older than our own time and place.

Most people enjoy some sense of permanence, even rather approving of the circumstance that old people eventually die (part of the permanence), until they themselves grow old. Children represent immortality, supposedly, and, to look at their scooting energy, they probably do. Their shouts are sufficient proof of that—shouts as harsh as a crow's cry that the next generation picks up at the age of five. Our image of ourselves throughout later life remains that of a person in his early twenties, old people say, and this may be part of the meaning of the vivid, monotonous schoolyard shouts. But much of my own feeling of permanence has been grounded in the wildness of the natural world. Wildness is permanence because it is what is unaltered, an infinity of particulars which are changing only very slowly without special reference to man. That the sun shines just as brightly on somebody who is dying in the desert of thirst is our good luck, because if he could turn out the sun for himself it would go out for us as well. Now, however, "wildness," instead of being infinity and superabundance, has a different reference: often simply the sniper gone haywire up in the bell tower. The glass panel in a taxicab that used to be there to protect the toffs from the unblanched opinions of the cabdriver is now intended to shield him from the violence of the toffs.

We don't know enough about what has been destroyed of the natural world even to take inventory; and though there should be other reasons besides what we call nature to believe in the permanence of the world, if nature in health and wealth and variety is to be permitted to exist only for its recreational value to man, then we must base our convictions about the world's permanence in the meanwhile, on the permanence of him. That wouldn't be so hard to do, when one considers people to be more good than bad, except for the exceptional power at hand nowadays in those brutal moments, even just to the local vandal. Ten years of good intentions can't match one night of cruelty; what we watch is the dangerously balanced duality. Where the Indians were spellbound by the succession of thunderheads in their sky—which was so much bigger than ours—we eye ourselves; or when we do turn our attention away from our own psyches, we watch our leaders, who have become bigger than the sky.

Looking at clergymen in the street, I notice the same inward stitching of worry in their faces that was characteristic of the profession when I went to church as a boy. It's like the face of a man at a sickbed when the patient has turned aside to his basin. The profession is in eclipse, almost in disrepute. First the civil-rights people wanted to know where the clergy had been for the past century or more; then the environmentalists wondered whether the clergy's sense of continuity extended only as far back as Christ's time. But clergymen have never claimed to be particularly prescient. They knew they weren't visionaries, but conventional fellows—good men at a sickbed—who tried to practice what everybody else preached, and who sorrowed about the same things a little bit more. They had not been much concerned with the lot of Negroes or the carnage in Vietnam until a larger constituency was; so, with the vulnerability of individuals who are both conventional and conscientious, they are quite rattled and feel blameworthy now.

The people with the fewest qualms are the evolutionists —those who remain evolutionists. Against most of the evidence of instability and disorientation, they proffer the same serviceable idea: that we have other lives to lead. Which is just what we always wished. To be married, yet take a vacation from marriage; to work and to loaf; to be kind and yet tough, rich yet idealistic; to live and to die.

We have our freedom and miraculous variance, and lately I've tried to discover which is the wildest mountain left in Vermont, from scouting as well as map-reading and talking to people. I think that I have. A jeep could bump to within a mile or two of the east or west base, but nobody happens to climb it. The mountains round about are encountered first, and it's an intricate, broad-topped, low little mountain, a confusion of starfish ridges and high swamps thick with windfalls. Nothing spectacular, no cliffs, waterfalls or fifty-mile views, just lots of forest. Its only distinction is its wildness, and moose, bear, lynx and coyotes make their homes there. I'm drawn to it and frequently wind toward it in walks, tasting the creeks that run off its sides, getting to know the valleys below, spending the night on mountains nearby so as to look at its contours at dusk and at dawn. Old log-skidding trails go halfway up, and I soft-foot up some of these, watching for animal prints, but though it seems like a low little mountain, hiding its higher complexities, eventually I turn back, postponing climbing clear to the top. Such an important event should not be rushed. If this indeed is the most remote mountain in Vermont, I hope to explore it gradually for many summers and never really climb it. Wildness is indifference, wildness exists without any knowledge of whether or not it will be destroyed. Its survival on this last mountain matters not to the mountain, nor to the attributes that define wildness, but only to me.

Half the battle is knowing what matters, and if we are prepared to make up our minds, an almost unlimited number of choices exists; in a way, the world is less crowded than it used to be. Alongside the closeness and safeness and sameness of modern living is a frightening roominess —cheap instant travel, swift risk and misery, old-fashioned loneliness and poverty, wars marbled with primeval terror, yet scholarship leading straight toward the roots of life, and so many experiments in pleasure in progress that it takes only a minimal gift for adventure for somebody to live several lives in the space of one. What is scandalous or impermissible now? Kicking a child in the street; maybe a few other odd taboos. So, what is happening is that we come to face the decision: do we want to explore ourselves in several marriages or in only one? Do we want one life to lead, or more? And how much does our own ambivalence really interest us? Is our self-concern the best focus in life? No doubt there aren't single answers; nor will our private answers necessarily have much to do with how we behave. Instead, as always, we trust that when we make a mistake we will land on our feet. What we know, as social sea changes come roaring at us, is that human beings are extraordinarily adaptive.

I stand on a pier near my house, looking at the river and south toward the larger harbor. If I were feeling glum it might seem an escape route, but I'm simply watching the sunlight jiggle on the wide currents, which are refreshingly broader than the yardsticks of distance that one is used to in the city. The water's jiggling and skittering establishes a parallel lightness in me, and though the weather happens to be cold, the sun's warm sheen brings out from within me, besides my good spirits, the lizards, snakes, turtles that I sprang from—all the creatures that merged to make me and that loved the sunlight, depending upon it so much that even if I no longer need it myself as imperatively, I can't feel it on my skin without slowing my thoughts and my feet, stopping and closing my eyes for a moment to *bask*.

So the day is lovely: there's sunshine that I turn my throat to slowly, the water hopping and sparkling, and many moiling dogs. Out of doors, the dogs too arouse a level of existence that is usually sleeping in me. It's as if I had grown from them and my feet were still linked to them, as if I were dangling my legs in the spaciousness of them. Fortunately for my own safety, however, I'm neither lizard nor dog, because this is the center of the city and two or three hundred people besides me are taking their ease on the pier. An inventory of what they look like could encompass the history of the world, which, needless to say, I'm not up to; but I'm at home with them. Without sparing much attention from the boats and the children, the lovers and girls and old people whose stories I'd like to hear, I can pretty well spot people in trouble or those who spell trouble, and can get a handle on anybody who ambles near. Schizophrenia, diabetic collapse, belt-between-the-teeth for epilepsy—subway things. There are encroachers and trapped people and people here before they go home to dress for a party. One can place them in their apartments and with their friends.

Hundreds of people, and a freighter steaming grandly by, and barges, tugboats, police boats, sightseers' launches. The West Side Highway provides constant engine static; and two private planes are crossing overhead, and now a 707, big, flat, gray as the newest invented metal, on a descent pattern, sweeping around toward LaGuardia Airport. A helicopter, too, is sliding downtown, very low and arrested-looking above us, with another angling in from New Jersey. From every direction aircraft are converging, it seems—I suddenly notice a third helicopter—and the trucks on West Street, and the roar of the cars on the highway over them, and some stunting guy in a powerboat making waves down where we are, and these crowds of wrought-up people here to relax for an hour. Lizard though I am, dog that I am, I am able to absorb it all. Somehow the more the merrier. I'm grinning. It's like swimming in the ocean, and suddenly Lake Superior is dumped in, then the Danube and Nile, then the Caspian Sea. One bobs above them. Whether one will always bob above them is a question. But, grinning, one finds that somehow each increment is adjusted for; one rides above it. It can all be absorbed.

About the Author

EDWARD HOAGLAND was born in New York City, grew up in Connecticut and graduated from Harvard in 1954. Soon afterwards, his first novel, *Cat Man*, appeared. At four-year intervals he published two more novels, *The Circle Home* and *The Peacock's Tail*, and a journal of his travels in northern British Columbia, *Notes From the Century Before*. In 1969 he turned to the essay form, and by now has written more than fifty, many of which were included in two previous collections, *The Courage of Turtles* and *Walking the Dead Diamond River* (see back of jacket).

Mr. Hoagland teaches or travels intermittently, and writes for a wide range of magazines. He is married, with a daughter of seven, and divides his time between New York City and Barton, Vermont.